THE
truth
ABOUT US

THE
truth
ABOUT US

A CALL TO CONFRONT BIAS, EMBRACE EMPATHY, AND BUILD A MORE INCLUSIVE WORLD

NONA LEE

press 49

Press 49
4980 South Alma School Road
Suite 2-493
Chandler, Arizona 85248

Volume pricing is available for bulk orders from corporations, associations, and others. For bulk order details and media inquiries, please get in touch with Press 49 at info@press49.com or 833.PRESS49 (833.773.7749).

FIRST EDITION

Library of Congress Control Number: 2025907298

ISBN (paperback): 978-1-953315-53-3
ISBN (eBook): 978-1-953315-54-0

SOC074000 SOCIAL SCIENCE / Diversity & Multiculturalism
SOC000000 SOCIAL SCIENCE / General
SOC023000 SOCIAL SCIENCE / Reference

Interior and cover design by Medlar Publishing Solutions Pvt Ltd., India
Printed in the United States of America

Dedication

This book is dedicated to the ancestors who have fought for my right to exist and to all who will come behind me.

"Until we are all free, we are none of us free."

—Emma Lazarus

Acknowledgments

For her unwavering support, encouragement to write this book, and contributions to it, I thank my friend and business coach, Deedra Determan. I also sincerely appreciate my colleagues David M. Dixon, S. Leigh Thompson, Bendita Cynthia Malakia, Stephen T. Kulp, and Dawna Callahan for their expertise and contributions to this book.

Special thanks to my publisher, Bridgett McGowen-Hawkins, for her expertise and keeping me on track. This book would not have been possible without the collaboration of Erika Winston, for whom I am deeply grateful.

A heartfelt thank you to my family and friends for allowing me to live my truth and loving me through it all.

This book is in memory of my first role model and shero, my "Gram," Ella Mae Norman, who showed me how to live, love, survive, and thrive in spaces where I have not always been welcome but where I know I belong. Thank you for your courage and inspiration.

Table of Contents

Section III – Understanding

Section IV – Taking Action

Section V – Humanity

Introduction

*"To reach that end goal you and I must be willing to be
straightforward with one another. We must be willing and
prepared to stare at ourselves in the mirror and speak the truth."*

—Mark Devro

How are you showing up in this world that we all share? This
is the question that I want you to keep in mind as you read
this book. For some of you, that won't be a problem at all, particularly if, like me, you are a member of one or more historically
marginalized groups navigating a society that was constructed with
the intention of excluding you. Doing so with any level of success
requires a constant awareness around the ways that you show up,
so the internal assessment that I request of you will likely not be
a problem.

For other readers, considering how you show up in the world
may feel unfamiliar, uncomfortable, and even a bit painful.

And that's because you may have never felt compelled to do so before. You are likely a member of the historically majority population, i.e., White cisgender males (and to some extent White cisgender females), whose inclusive existence in this world does not hinge on your ability to show up in a way that society finds "acceptable." You probably didn't grow up hearing that you must work twice as hard to get half as far or enter the workforce, terrified that your colleagues would discover your sexual orientation. Exclusion likely was not part of your daily experience, but I ask you to take a different perspective as you read through these pages.

It is my hope that as you read this book, you will think back to how you chose to show up or not show up in the past. Then, carefully consider how you are showing up in the present and allow your mind to expand around how you can show up in the future. Think about how you want to show up in this world and who you want to be as a person of influence and leadership. Think about the world you want your kids to live in and your role in making that a reality. And think about the beauty of learning more about people who differ from you, people whose value is equivalent to yours, simply because they are living, breathing, feeling human beings. Perfectly imperfect. Just as we all are.

My name is Nona Lee. I am the founder and CEO of Truth DEI Consulting, a consulting firm helping organizations determine current and future growth opportunities and strategies in diversity, equity, and inclusion (DEI). My professional experience has included various leadership roles within the sports industry, including serving as the first executive vice president and chief legal officer for the Arizona Diamondbacks Major League Baseball

(MLB) franchise. I was one of only three or four women to hold this position with an MLB club, and to my knowledge, I was the only openly gay person to do so.

After the murder of George Floyd, I very much wanted to be front and center of the equal justice protests. Unfortunately, the need for a spinal fusion kept me from doing so, but watching the commitment of the protestors impacted me incredibly. They cared, even though many of them had no personal experience with the impact of police brutality on Black males in America. Those young kids were putting themselves on the line to solve a problem they did not create. Upon witnessing that, I knew that I could no longer sit back and do nothing, which, in my mind, made me a part of that problem. Yes, I had crafted a professional path of being "the first" in many influential ways, and that was incredibly important within the sports world—I was deeply grateful for all the opportunities that led me there. However, as much as I loved it, my role in professional sports seemed small compared to the possibility of changing hearts and minds so that all people could feel safe and lead equitable lives.

DEI, or EDI as defined by the American Psychological Association, "is a conceptual framework that promotes fair treatment and full participation of all people, especially populations that have historically been underrepresented or subject to discrimination because of their background, identity, disability, etcetera. Equity involves providing resources according to …need….Diversity refers to the representation or composition of various social identity groups in a work group, organization, or community. In other words, diversity is a fact. Inclusion strives for an environment that offers affirmation, celebration, and appreciation of different approaches, styles, perspectives, and experiences."[1] In other words, at its core, DEI is about all of us. DEI provided me with an opportunity to drive the changes that I wanted to see in the world. It offered a platform to show up differently and contribute to creating a more inclusive society where differences are not only acknowledged but celebrated. I found a meaningful way to align my personal values with my business acumen for the development of more equitable work environments because DEI is not only the right thing to do—it is also a business imperative that impacts the bottom line.

Having been in many corporate environments, I knew the greatest impact of speaking to organizational leaders, and that is who I speak to in the pages of this book. As a decision-maker, you significantly influence the culture and norms of your workplace culture. You set the standard for other leaders to follow, and that example influences upper management, supervisors, and the workforce as a whole. Many of the anecdotes and examples I offer will be through the lens of the workplace. Still, because I also recognize that we cannot separate the workplace from people's personal experiences, there will be some personal stories to fully illustrate the TRUTH concept. That's part of the problem we are seeing now. People fail to see one another as people, so they don't think about what they experience.

When I decided to start a DEI consulting business, I knew unequivocally what it would be called. TRUTH came to me as a clear and powerful reminder that unless we are all willing to confront the truth about ourselves—where we are personally, in our organizations, and in society—we will never be able to heal and move forward. There can be no transformation without first embracing the truth, but are you, as an individual or organization, willing to do that?

Are you willing to accept your lack of awareness? Are you willing to look in the mirror and acknowledge the learned behaviors contributing to your biases and perspectives? As a business leader, are you willing to look closely at your company and receive honest feedback about what the people in (and outside) your organization see and feel regarding DEI? Are you willing to move forward despite the discomfort that sometimes comes with acknowledging the truth about who you are as an organization? Are you willing to be like Costco and Delta Airlines and resist the urge to shrink and acquiesce to people, usually White men in particular, who are uncomfortable with change and criticize your efforts as a waste of time?

Think about when a problem arises in a marital relationship. No matter how hard you try to ignore it, the underlying issue does not just go away. You actually have to address it or get help doing so if you do not want the marriage to fail. DEI is no different. We cannot move on and get to a better place of healing until we confront the issues that continue to exist within ourselves and in our communities and workplaces.

We have a difficult history around our treatment of people who are different. It is not one of love, kindness, and respect. It's a history of disregard and disrespect, with generations of people choosing to look away and ignore the world's injustices. That privilege of unawareness has resulted in an environment where we have failed to help one another thrive in our workplaces, our communities, and our society.

The truth is that we will all be members of an underserved community at some point in our lives. If you are lucky, you will be elderly one day, at which point you may experience a turn of events that leaves you needing some type of assistance. When that day comes, and you understand the pain of being unseen and unsupported, will you be able to look back and say that you cared about individuals who needed DEI assistance when you didn't?

At Truth DEI, we work within the framework of the word TRUTH, which we use as an acronym for helping our clients first understand what their *Truth* is and embrace it; *Reconcile* that truth in order to get to a place of *Understanding*; and *Take Action* while seeing people through the lens of *Humanity* instead of ignoring their realities. These principles guide the direction of this book. It is not about guilt or shame. It's about being mindful of our empathy and recognizing that *the truth just is*—and if you don't want it to be, how can you do better? The bottom line is that treating people with respect and valuing them is simply the right thing to do.

My journey has been one of adversity, but I transparently share it in this book to inspire you to take action. In the pages that follow, you will also meet some of my colleagues in the DEI space, amazing professionals who have spent years working to create a world where all people are seen, considered, and cared for. In addition to their professional truths, each of them has personal truths that have informed their work in incredible ways. I offer their contributions to expand your perspective and knowledge about the wide-reaching moral case for DEI and its incredible impact on all people as members of diverse communities, allies, business leaders, decision-makers, and most importantly, people with a shared humanity.

People from historically underrepresented groups have a heavy price to pay, and we pay it every single day in our struggles to succeed in a world that was not only not made for us but was made to keep us from thriving and succeeding. We fight through these challenges while also dealing with the reality that many people who do not share our experiences are in denial about what we go through. These are the same people who believe laws and words on a piece of paper have adequately addressed discrimination and inequity. But progress comes from what we decide to do as human beings. We cannot count on politicians to make this world better for all of us. We must rely on one another.

I hope you walk away from this book feeling a connection between your heart and mind that inspires you to do the work. I did not write this book solely to inspire people from diverse communities. I wrote it to inspire everyone. I want to send a message that your choices now can help create a world where equity and inclusion just are—with no need for further conversations.

SECTION I

Truth

CHAPTER ONE

The Truth About Us as Individuals

I was born in December 1959. I always include the month because being closer to 1960 somehow makes me feel younger. I grew up in Los Angeles, California, in a neighborhood where being Black set me apart at a very young age. People constantly questioned my dad's ethnicity, assuming that he was Mexican or Italian because of his light skin and straighter hair. I remember my dad telling me that when he went into the Navy, they described him as White on his enlistment papers, even though he told them that he was Black. He fought hard to have them change his race to Negro because my dad was incredibly proud of who he was.

My mom, although not very dark-skinned, was obviously Black. She said that when I was born at Queen of Angels Hospital in Los Angeles, the nurses tried to keep her from leaving the hospital with me because they thought that my skin was far too light for it to be possible for me to belong to her.

My dad looked very much like my grandfather, who also could have passed for White if he'd chosen to (he never did). Like my father, he also married a brown-skinned Black woman, so it was a very similar situation to my parents. I don't know where the intersection with Black and White first began in my family or how far back it goes, but growing up with light skin and wavy hair, under others' false assumption that I was biracial, proved to be an interesting and sometimes difficult childhood.

We were the only Black family when we first moved into our southwest Los Angeles neighborhood, which was incredibly controversial then. I was only a couple of years old, but I remember being terrified one night when White teenagers drove their car across our front lawn, throwing bottles at our house and yelling horrible things at us. This was just the beginning of my encounters with racism.

When my sister and I were old enough to leave my parents, we were sent to Natchez, Mississippi, to spend the summers with my dad's family. I remember noticing the different treatment my sister and I received from the clerks at the grocery store. They always treated us more politely than our darker-skinned cousins, and that really bothered me. While playing outside with our cousins one day, Grandma Susie rushed us all into the house. As I got up to go inside, I looked over my left shoulder and saw a group of people coming down Franklin Street toward my grandparents' house. Some were on horseback, some were walking, and all were dressed from head to toe in white. When I got in the house, I asked my grandmother who these people were. She explained that they were the KKK and that they didn't like us and may hurt us because of the color of our skin. My world was forever changed by the realization that there were people in this world who didn't even know me, who hated me, and who would hurt me just because of the color of my skin. This shocking and puzzling awakening still mystifies me to this day. There is absolutely no good, legitimate, or logical reason why White people believe they are superior to me; they just decided they are and are loath to let go of that idea at any cost. Frankly, it has always made me grateful not to be White and even prouder to be Black.

Over time, like so many other suburban communities of the sixties, White flight changed the demographics of my Los Angeles neighborhood as White families moved out and families of color moved in. As a child, I didn't know that systematic policies pushed those changes in my neighborhood. I just knew I had new friends, and some of them looked like me. My dad had a hard time with some of the Black teenage boys who moved into the neighborhood, though. They would walk across his lawn and say things to him about his light skin, and I used to worry for them because my dad had a temper. He was not a person to mess with because you never knew what might set him off. I remember one afternoon, he stood on the front porch with a shotgun, waiting for them to come by. This time, they kept walking silently by. There was no encounter, and I don't recall my dad ever having a problem with them again.

Growing up was challenging and confusing. I always knew I was loved in my house and by my family and extended family, but anything outside the family and my few neighborhood friends made me feel unsafe. When I joined my sister (who was a year ahead of me) in high school at St. Mary's Academy in Inglewood,

California, we took the city bus to and from school until my sister was old enough to drive. I dreaded taking the bus home because we were always picked on by other Black kids who taunted us for thinking we were better than them because of our light skin and wavy hair. So, it didn't take long for me to feel the sting of rejection as the other Black girls bullied my sister and me. I didn't understand or appreciate what they were saying because I did not feel that way at all, but I was told untruths about myself on a daily basis.

MY POWER

When I was ten years old, I found refuge in the pool of the Inglewood YMCA, where I learned to swim. I quickly advanced through all the lessons and began helping teach the toddlers. I felt so free and at home in the pool. There was something safe about the solitude and peace of the water. The other joy of swimming was completely immersing myself in my competitive nature. I felt empowered to compete and to be the best. The pool was where I found my power and a connection to myself that I had been missing.

Understanding my passion for swimming, my dad found an Amateur Athletic Union (AAU) swimming team and asked me if I wanted to try out. I immediately said yes. So, at twelve years old, I tried out for the Hawthorne Otters AAU swim team. I remember being so intimidated walking into that tryout. There were a lot of kids there, and it wasn't lost to me that they were all White, except for four Filipino sisters who were already on the team. But even through the feelings of intimidation, I was ready to compete for a spot. After I completed my tryout, the coach told me that I made the team and to come back the next day for practice. I was so proud and excited. Trying out had been a scary experience, and my success made me feel so accomplished.

I walked into practice the next day and noticed fewer kids than the previous day. Many of my White teammates were gone, and many of those who remained were very standoffish toward me. The Filipino girls were among a very small group who made me feel welcome. After practice, my dad told me that some of the parents wouldn't let their children continue with the team because they didn't want them swimming with me, a Black child. I was so hurt and confused by that. It was the same hurt and confusion that I felt when my grandmother told me about the KKK.

I could not understand why anyone would have a problem with me. I didn't do anything to them. I only wanted to swim, just like they did. This was not the 1960s in the Deep South. This was the early 1970s in the supposedly progressive city of L.A. I felt like I was growing up in a world where I didn't belong anywhere. Black people shunned me for not being Black enough, and White people shunned me for being too Black. It's not an uncommon story, but it is a story that comes with a lot of pain. I didn't know where I belonged, and I felt rejection from all sides.

After learning about the other kids quitting the team, a part of me considered not going back. When I told my father I did not want to be where I wasn't wanted, he responded by asking me if I wanted to swim. When I said that I did, he told me that I had earned the right to be there, and if I wanted to swim, I would stay on the team, which is precisely what I did. My dad took me to practice every day, and he eventually became an unofficial assistant coach of the team. I stayed with that team for three years, but it took a while to feel like I truly belonged. I was one of the better swimmers on the team, which helped a lot. I guess I proved myself enough to be accepted.

I continued to excel in the pool, and I loved every minute of it. I practiced for two hours every day after school and quickly moved up through the competitive skill brackets. I earned a National Champion medal in the Junior Olympics 50-meter freestyle at fourteen. An Olympic-level coach who saw me swim extended an invitation for me to train with him, but it would require my parents to sell the house and relocate to what would be another all-White community. I can't say for sure that it had anything to do with my decision not to continue swimming, but I was uncomfortable asking my parents to make that kind of change. To be honest, there was some fear, too. What if I didn't make the Olympic team after asking them to make such a huge sacrifice? It was a lot for a young teenager to decide, and I wasn't ready to have that weight on my shoulders. That decision has become one of my biggest regrets. Sometimes, I still question what could have happened if I had gone. Would I be an Olympian? From then on, I decided never to let fear keep me from doing things. Even now, I intentionally do things I'm afraid to because I don't want to let fear win.

Once I stopped swimming, I placed all my focus on basketball, which I had also been playing competitively since elementary school. I started by playing with my brother, who is eleven years older than me. Born from my dad's first marriage, he grew up in Mississippi. He played basketball in high school (where he was the first Black student at the school) and college. When he would come to stay with us over the holidays and school breaks, he and my cousins would play basketball in the backyard on a hoop my father put up by the garage. After some pleading on my part, my brother would let me play with them, and I just fell in love with the game.

My elementary school started a girls' basketball team when I was eleven. I joined, but I didn't like it initially because it wasn't the game I loved to play in the backyard with my brother. There were these ridiculous rules that girls could only dribble twice and stop. And certain positions were not allowed to go past half-court. I knew it wasn't how the boys played, and I could not understand why we had to play differently. Eventually, the rules for girls changed to the traditional game, and I started to love being on the court. I juggled basketball and swimming until I decided to leave the pool behind and concentrate on the court.

I attended St. Mary's Academy, a private all-girls Catholic school in Inglewood, and made the team my first year. I really appreciated that team experience, especially having come from a situation where I didn't feel connected or safe with people outside of my immediate group of friends or cousins. Basketball helped me learn how to build relationships with people outside of that limited experience and still feel safe. It taught me skills that translated into the workplace. I learned how to be a part of the team and that everybody brings something of value to the court. I learned to care about and trust my teammates to do their jobs.

During my junior year of high school, I met Desiree Marcelin, who was a year ahead of me. She wanted to play on the team, but for some reason, the coach wouldn't let her. I talked the coach into letting her play, and Desi went on to get recruited by Pepperdine University. I didn't get recruited out of high school, but I wanted to keep playing with Desi, so I applied to Pepperdine, got accepted, and walked on to the team. After my freshman/walk-on year, I earned a scholarship to help offset my educational expenses.

I grew up believing that I was not good enough or smart enough. But in the space of sports, I felt good enough for the first time and smart enough and strong enough. I felt like I belonged, which is where my power came from. Sports have been my saving grace, where I found my courage, determination, and ability to stand independently and take risks. It is the way I connect to the world and myself.

BEING "NORMAL"

My first wonderings about being different from other girls happened in the first or second grade. I felt an attraction to Sister Angela at my Catholic elementary school, and I didn't really understand what it was. I was always a tomboy and never had any interest in the things that most little girls seemed to love so much. Whenever my parents would give me a doll, I would typically take its head off to figure out how it was made.

As I got older, I had friends who were boys who I played with all the time and friends who were girls that I played with sometimes. But occasionally, I would have a friend or meet someone new to whom I felt an attraction. I thought it was common for everyone because I couldn't identify the feeling. Further into my teens, I started to understand that I was attracted to girls. But I also knew that it wasn't considered acceptable.

My mom was a legal secretary for an entertainment lawyer, and a couple of gay men worked in the office with her. I remember hearing my father speak badly about them at the dinner table, using awful words. I would feel such shame. Being a tomboy was met with some resistance from my mother. I remember wanting a skateboard, but she insisted I get roller skates instead. She also threatened to send me to charm school at one point. But my dad and I bonded over my tomboy ways. We played sports together, and I would help him work on the car in the driveway. Those connections made us buddies, which was important to me because I wanted so badly to have his approval. He was a tough guy who put a lot of pressure on us to succeed, but I also got to see another side of him through our mutual love for sports. It was a space where I could feel safe with him.

I don't know if my parents suspected anything during my childhood. I tried to live a "normal" life with "normal" experiences, which included boyfriends and dating guys. I did like them. They were nice, but I was never attracted to them in the same way I was attracted to girls. My truth in dealing with my sexuality at a young age is that it was awful. It was isolating and lonely with a lot of guilt attached to it. The shame I experienced about the feelings I could not control created yet another space where I did not feel comfortable or safe. I began to think that being gay was an awful thing, but I also knew that I had really strong feelings that could not be ignored.

MY INDIVIDUAL TRUTHS

I started this book with my childhood story because I believe that is where our truth begins. The color of my skin, the texture of my hair, the feelings in my heart. These things that I had no control over fueled the hatred that I encountered as a child.

Though I have tried hard to process and grow from these experiences, seeds were planted that still impact me today. I routinely take the Harvard Implicit Association Test (IAT) to check my own biases. When I first took the IAT, I was surprised to learn that I had a slight bias in favor of lighter-skinned people. I was tempted to disagree because I think darker skin is so beautiful and often wish I was much darker. But the results made me examine my own truths and how they still affect me today.

Colorism was a part of my truth from the day the nuns at the Queen of Angels Hospital tried to keep my mom from taking me home. Though always well-intended, my mom fed into it every time she told me and my sister how pretty we were with our light skin and "good" hair. It showed up as internalized racism and diminished self-worth when the Black girls at school bullied me. My IAT results made me question whether I internalized what was being told to me and if I bought into the stereotypes fed into me by my mother and those grocery clerks in Natchez, Mississippi.

My bias is something that I have to be mindful of as I continue to reconcile my childhood. I've always had this deep desire to be comfortably part of the Black community, which never truly happened for me. During my high school years, I began to feel unwelcome, and the bullying made me feel unsafe, which is an ongoing theme that has followed me since then. I didn't feel safe in the Black community. I didn't feel safe in the White community. At times, I didn't even feel safe at home.

I loved and appreciated my dad, but he was an angry man who would lose his temper; I was never sure what might set him off. I remember one day, while we were play-wrestling, as we often did, something triggered him, and he started to strike me for real. I could not understand what had happened as I felt the pain of my own father's punches. But when I looked up into his eyes, they looked completely empty, as if nobody was home. I can't remember what happened to make him stop, but my mom arrived home to me standing in the hall in my pajamas and my dad sitting at the kitchen table with his suitcase packed. He told my mother that he was leaving because of what he had done to me, but my mom pleaded with him to stay. I needed protection from my mother at that moment, and she did not give it to me.

I think that is part of what led me to the work that I do now. I am still trying to feel safe and like I belong in a world where I haven't felt any of those things. But I also want to provide a safe space for all of us to feel included and valued. The truth of the matter is that it really isn't that hard. Providing a safe space does not require much more than being kind, compassionate, and accepting people for who they are. My individual truths have shaped who I am, and I continually work to eliminate my own biases as I champion DEI each and every day.

CHAPTER TWO

The Truth About Humanity

*"The greatness of humanity is not in being human,
but in being humane."*

—Mahatma Gandhi

Humans are social beings. We desire meaningful relationships and want to feel a sense of belonging. We thrive in an environment where we are embraced for who we are, even if who we are is different from those around us. We want to be seen as individuals who deserve empathy, respect, and understanding. And we want to be given equitable opportunities to love and live in a way that makes us feel happy and complete.

This is the basis of humanity, traits that we all share as human beings. Yet, though we all have a desire for these needs to be met, far too many of us choose to ignore or even deny these needs in others. We take away the humanity of others because they have some characteristic, thought, or feeling that differs from our own. Sometimes, that hate is rooted in something so deep that we lose the capacity to see people as human beings or care about how they're impacted, whether it's by microaggression, emotional harm, or physical harm up to and including death. Inhumanity has lasting effects, conditioning generations to live in fear and apprehension. It impacts us all.

Watching the news each evening, it feels like we have never before been more divided as a human race. But inhumanity has a long history. Some scientists suggest that the first violent precursors to what we label as warfare today happened ten thousand years ago on the continent of Africa. From the beginning of time, humans have found differences to separate ourselves from "others," seeing people who are in some way different as "them" versus "us." It creates a divide, usually for the purpose of making the "othered" group feel excluded or even devalued.

THE INHUMANITY OF OTHERING

We have all seen othering play out in our lives, whether we were the targets, the perpetrators, or bystanders who chose to stay silent. As a child, I was othered when I sought to be a member of the competitive swimming team and again when my classmates decided my skin was too light for their definition of Black. That was my experience as a young lawyer when older White male lawyers would ask me to get their coffee and even later in my legal career when my

White male colleagues went to lunch together nearly every day—very rarely, if ever, inviting me.

Even at its most subtle level, othering can send a powerful message of "You're not like us, so you don't fit in," impacting individuals, groups, and society as a whole. When we treat people as others, we take away their humanity, creating a sense of isolation and damaging their self-esteem. Over time, they can experience anxiety, depression, and a feeling of disconnection.

In the group context, othering fosters division and mistrust, creating an "us versus them" dynamic, where the "in-group" is privileged while the "out-group" faces the burdens that come along with exclusion and marginalization. It dismisses the contributions of entire groups, silencing valuable perspectives, creativity, and innovation while simultaneously creating thought echo chambers where members of the "in-group" exist with little to no understanding of the people they share this earth with.

These are the building blocks of systemic inequities, where opportunities, resources, and rights are distributed inequitably based on arbitrary differences like race, gender, or ability. Othering destabilizes our communities and perpetuates cycles of division, making it harder for us to trust one another. That lack of connection is what leads to those heartbreaking images of social unrest and violence on our screens.

The prejudice and hatred that stems from othering persists across generations, reinforcing harmful ideologies and perpetuating systemic injustice. Segregation, colonialism, and disenfranchisement are all rooted in the historical practice of othering entire groups of people, and that separation is often manifested in brutal ways.

Nearly thirteen million African people were stolen from their land and forced into enslavement between 1501 and 1867 during the Transatlantic Slave Trade.[1] For those who were brought to the eastern shores of America, slaveholders placed monetary value on their lives based on their perceived physical abilities. Men were auctioned off along with livestock and even inanimate household goods. Women were valued solely based on their ability to bear and rear children, perverting the human essence of motherhood into a commodity.

On the plantation, the enslaved were forced to endure the severity of their working conditions. They picked cotton from sunup to sundown as blood trickled from their fingers and bare feet. Their only worth was their ability to perform manual duties in the field and inside the master's home. Women were forced into sexual relations with enslavers with the resulting offspring ignored and treated as enslaved people despite the societal status of their biological fathers. Enslaved men also faced sexual oppression, forced to reproduce for the purpose of creating new generations of labor.

Even laws supported the inhumanity of enslaved people as property and allowed for the violence inflicted against them. The Fugitive Slave Act was a federal law that permitted the capture and return of runaway enslaved people within the United States.[2] Not only did it direct local governments to capture and return escapees to their owners, but it also imposed penalties on anyone who aided an enslaved person in their escape. The atrocities against enslaved Africans in America were thought by those less aware and/or concerned to have ended with the issuance of the Emancipation Proclamation on January 1, 1863. For the enslaved in Galveston, Texas, that certainly was not the case, as they were not told of their free-dom for more than two years later on June 19, 1865, celebrated now as Juneteenth.

Even today, vestiges of slavery live on in our society, our com-munities, and our workplaces. Some of the world's most powerful and profitable corporations still benefit from the capital originated by the Transatlantic Slave Trade.

THE INHUMANITY OF REMOVAL

The act of cruelly and viciously killing someone goes against our innate sense of right versus wrong as human beings. People find it much easier to inflict horror on another when they do not see their victims as people. Removing someone's humanity permits perpetrators of harm to view their victims as nothing more than dangerous or pesty animals, and we have seen examples of this throughout history.

Enslaved Africans were reduced to property, deemed suitable for theft and purchase. Nazis commonly referred to Jewish people as rats and vermin while carrying out the atrocities of the Holocaust. The Hutu tribe of Rwanda called members of the Tutsi tribe cockroaches while committing rapes, kidnappings, and murders during the Rwandan genocide. And the Indigenous populations of North America were characterized as savages in order to justify the brutality leveraged against them.

European colonists systematically conquered and eliminated tens of millions of North American native people through physical and biological warfare. With a belief in the inferiority of native cultures and customs, colonists labeled native people as savages, denoting an absence of humanity, reason, or values. The Bear River Massacre of 1863 has been characterized as one of the deadliest slaughters of indigenous people in American history.[3] The Shoshone Nation was a tribe of more than 17,000 people that resided across parts of Nevada, Utah, Idaho, and Wyoming. During the 1800s, settler movement into Shoshone land caused major clashes. In January of 1863, an estimated 350 Shoshone people were killed when US soldiers opened fire on the entire tribe, most of whom were only armed with tomahawks, bows, and arrows. Generations to come would be told stories of the white snow turning red with blood.

This disregard for the humanity of Native Americans was a consistent part of American history. As the country expanded in territory, indigenous people were driven out and removed to designated areas. With no regard for their histories, cultures, or customs, they were forced away from the lands that their ancestors had inhabited for hundreds of years—long before the "founding of America" by colonists. In 1851, the Indian Appropriations Act created the reservation system, officially relocating tribes onto farming reservations with the main purpose of bringing Native Americans under the control of the US government.[4] The humanity of Native Americans and their right to govern themselves was replaced with a paternalistic system of regulation that has stifled the health and wealth of tribes for decades. Reservations include more than fifty million acres of land, yet only about five percent of it is owned by private individuals.[5]

Land was not the only sense of humanity stolen from Native American tribes. Established in the 1950s, the Indian Adoption Project forced the adoption of Native American children into non-Native families. Scholars suggest that twenty-five to thirty-five percent of Native American children were taken from their communities and given to White families.[6] This inhumane disregard for family continued until the passage of the Indian Child Welfare Act of 1978.[7] Yet, despite the passage of federal law, the devastating impact of the treatment of the Native American community for hundreds of years persists as Native Americans continue to seek equity within a land that refuses to fully acknowledge their humanity.

The Holocaust is another tragic example of what can happen when one group of people decides to dehumanize another group of people through removal—when othering is taken to its most destructive form. Between 1933 and 1945, approximately six million European Jewish people were persecuted and murdered under the state-sponsored direction of the Nazi German regime.[8] Led by Adolf Hitler, the government promoted a nationalist ideology based on theories of biological superiority of an "Aryan master race" and nationalized antisemitism. Nazi Germans abducted more than ten million people from various European countries, forcing them into extreme living conditions with severe mistreatment, malnutrition, and abuse, leading to horrendous deaths.

In an attempt to justify their horrendous actions, the Nazis spread propaganda labeling Jews and other groups as fundamentally different and inferior. They depicted the Nazi government as heroically "restoring order" against "subhuman creatures" that threatened the Aryan race. German newspapers used caricatures to deny the humanity of

21

Jewish people and portray them as animals. Over time, these dehumanization strategies led to the societal acceptance of Jewish people being forcibly removed from their communities and murdered in mass numbers. By dehumanizing entire groups of people, the Nazis justified actions that would otherwise have been unthinkable.

David Livingstone Smith authored a book entitled *Less Than Human*, where he discusses the significant role that dehumanization plays in carrying out cruelty and genocide against fellow human beings. In an interview on NPR's *Talk of the Nation*, he explained how this mindset allows human beings "to overcome the very deep and natural inhibitions they have against treating other people like game animals or vermin or dangerous predators." He went on to state, "When the Nazis described Jews as Untermenschen, or subhumans, they didn't mean it metaphorically. They didn't mean they were like subhumans. They meant they were literally subhuman."[9]

The United States Holocaust Memorial Museum defines *antisemitism* as a prejudice against or hatred of Jews.[10] It is hatred that can take many forms and show up within our society subtly and violently. From employment and housing discrimination to senseless attacks on the lives of Jewish people, antisemitism has an extensive history within American society.

Members of the Jewish community in North America continue to be the subject of disparate treatment. On October 27, 2018, Robert D. Bowers walked into Pittsburgh's Tree of Life synagogue and opened fire on a congregation of worshiping people, yelling, "All Jews must die!"[11] This horrific act of anti-Semitic violence resulted in the deaths of eleven people and injured six others, making it one of the deadliest attacks on the Jewish community in US history and one tragedy in a growing trend of increasing violence against Jewish communities in recent years.

The inhumanity of removal is also evident in the broad erasure of the fundamental rights that have been long and hard fought. Rights that were upheld to finally give people some sense of humanity within a society where colonizers systematically made themselves the priority over everything and everyone. Between 1942 and 1945, thousands of people of Japanese descent, including US citizens, were removed from their homes, their businesses, and their communities, incarcerated in crowded detention camps.[12] This horrific violation of American civil rights was carried out through an executive order under US President Theodore Roosevelt, and many believed it implausible that such a tragedy could happen again. However, the Trump administration has used—and continues to use—the the same executive order strategy to orchestrate the removal of immigrants without due process.

Even as an American citizen born and raised in the United States, witnessing these acts of inhumanity creates fears that I could also be removed based on the whim of a political leader. Under the second Trump administration, I have found myself questioning what being an American citizen actually means. If I'm not deemed so in the eyes of people in power, how will that impact my life and my liberties?

THE INHUMANITY OF HATRED

The strategy of stripping away the humanity of an entire group has long been a weapon in the arsenal to marginalize the LGBTQ+

community. It operates by portraying LGBTQ+ individuals as fundamentally irreconcilable with societal norms, constructing an "us versus them" mindset, where heterosexual and cisgender identities are labeled as the default of "normal," and LGBTQ+ identities are characterized as deviant.

German law criminalized homosexuality as far back as 1871, but these laws were rarely enforced until Hitler took power.[13] Nazis arrested thousands of LGBTQ+ individuals, primarily gay men, and forced them into concentration camps where they received the harshest treatment. To ensure their ostracization and further dehumanization, gay men were forced to wear shirts with a downward-pointing pink triangle sewn onto them, intended as a symbol of shame. Even after the conclusion of World War II, many gay men remained incarcerated under Germany's anti-gay laws until the early 1970s.

In the United States, anti-gay rhetoric began early in the colonies due in part to the heavy influence of Puritan and Christian norms. Homosexuality, or sodomy, was routinely outlawed among the early colonies, with the first documented prosecution for lesbian sexual behavior occurring in 1649. These laws remained on the books of most US states well into the twentieth century.

In 1969, New York City police officers raided a gay bar in Greenwich Village called Stonewall Inn. These types of unjustified raids on gay establishments were common. Still, on this particular night, some of the patrons decided to actively resist, leading to a three-day demonstration against police harassment and brutality that came to be known as Stonewall. However, though Stonewall is one of the most infamous early examples of twentieth-century violence against gay and queer people in the United States, it is far from the only incident.

For years, terms like "lifestyle choice" have been used to frame LGBTQ+ identities as unnatural or even threatening. Historically, laws criminalizing homosexuality or barring same-sex marriage codified LGBTQ+ people as outsiders who didn't deserve the same protections or privileges as others. Socially, we see it play out as exclusion from families, communities, and cultural narratives. They are often made to feel invisible or unwelcome in spaces where their identities are ignored or invalidated.

The harm of this inhumane, hateful behavior can be profound, isolating LGBTQ+ individuals and ultimately leading to higher rates of depression, homelessness, and violence. Societally, it creates divides so vast that most people do not even attempt genuine understanding. Disregarding the humanity of gay people has been as formally ingrained into American history as sexism and racism. Accounts of LGBTQ violence—especially against the transgender community at this time—are heartbreakingly familiar with senseless murder, assault, and rape, fueling the fear that many gay people have around living their truths, both within the workplace and out in society, forced instead to always undertake the exhausting work of hiding parts of themselves.

THE PSYCHOLOGICAL IMPACT OF INHUMANITY

Post-traumatic stress disorder (PTSD) is a mental health problem that develops after going through or witnessing a terrifying or highly stressful event. While an emotional reaction is normal under stressful circumstances, if it lasts longer than a few weeks and causes problems in other areas of a person's life, it is likely PTSD. According to studies conducted by the National Institutes of Health, experiencing discrimination or harassment can negatively impact both physical and mental health, causing psychological and physiological stresses that accumulate over time and lead to harmful health outcomes and health-related behaviors. Even the anticipation of mistreatment can cause harm and significantly impact a person's ability to thrive.

When the humanity of a person is constantly threatened, they are forced to endure repeated traumas, which can lead to PTSD over time. They may feel a constant sense of danger, even in common everyday environments, because the otherness that they have endured has taught them to constantly anticipate harm or judgment. Think about the nervousness that a transgender woman may feel in an environment where violence against transgender women is at an all-time high. This state of hypervigilance is a form of PTSD. Being dehumanized can also make people feel less worthy, deepening feelings of shame, hopelessness, and isolation, which can all be symptoms of PTSD.

But it's not only the people harmed by these behaviors who suffer. Being responsible for the harm caused to another human being, especially when forced to do so by an authority figure, can also result in lasting trauma. There may be residual psychological effects through guilt or societal reckoning. Suppose the individual chooses to confront and reject those behaviors in the future.

In that case, they may face ostracism, backlash, or even threats from their community, also potentially resulting in stress and trauma.

Even being exposed to inhumane treatment can have lasting impacts on a person's psyche. Whether the treatment witnessed was as large-scale as genocide or on a small scale, such as a microaggression, everyone involved may feel the effect at some level. People are not naturally programmed to ignore the humanity of one another. When these events happen in front of their eyes, they can leave mental and emotional scars on the witnesses.

SEEING EACH OTHER'S HUMANITY

The truth about humanity is that we, as individuals, have different experiences that shape who we are. These historical incidents exemplify that sometimes we don't see or treat each other as individual human beings. We see each other as groups based on stereotypes driven by misinformation, fear, and hate. We don't stop to think about the legacy that people continue to carry every day based upon historical inequities. Just because a group has survived an event doesn't mean they are okay. It doesn't mean that they are thriving. It doesn't mean they have access to the same opportunities as everyone else. We have to stop looking away and start looking at each other and really seeing each other—seeing each other's humanity—in order to have a truly inclusive world.

Reconciliation

CHAPTER THREE

The Truth About Society

We, as people, generally have the capacity and ability to do amazing things, including caring about other people and showing them tremendous compassion. But when we get caught up in our circumstances, at best, we ignore what is happening with other people in the world, and, at worst, we engage in behavior to the detriment of other people.

Reconciliation involves unlearning the harmful behaviors behind historical and societal injustices and dismantling the structures that uphold them. It is crucial in fostering environments that value diversity, prioritize equity, and evolve inclusion into the norm. It challenges the learned behaviors at the foundation of systemic ideologies, like White supremacy and patriarchy, that are embedded into our society and institutions.

LEARNED BEHAVIORS

Society is shaped by a multitude of learned behaviors acquired through socialization and interaction within a community. These behaviors influence how individuals think, act, and relate to one another, ultimately building the structure of society as a whole. We establish cultural norms and determine acceptable behaviors based on a shared sense of underlying values, but those norms and values are neither monolithic nor innate. They are learned through socialization agents like family upbringing, peer interactions, and in today's complex society, social media. Learned behaviors teach individuals what they think is expected of them in order to function within society. Sometimes, they function for the betterment of society; sometimes, they do not. And wrapped up in all of that is the truth about society.

The biases and systemic injustices we witness in society are closely connected to the learned behaviors that impact our development from the start. From a very young age, our families provide our first exposure to attitudes and beliefs through their instructions and observations. Those examples shape our values and movement through the world, and if the lessons are racist, sexist, homophobic, or otherwise judgmental of people who are in any way "different," children are likely to internalize those attitudes as normal and acceptable and carry them into their societal interactions.

These behaviors can be further embedded as children progress into young adults, especially when their peer groups share the same biased attitudes or beliefs, which is often the case in nondiverse geographic locations. Suppose the majority of people in a community outwardly communicate negative feelings about particular groups of people. In that case, chances are high that those attitudes will perpetuate prejudice and reinforce stereotypical beliefs among young, impressionable minds. Social acceptance of discriminatory behaviors reinforces the belief that these biased values are appropriate and the norm.

Education is another influential socialization factor due to the sheer amount of time students spend in school settings. Schools act as more than just centers for academic instruction; they play a vital role in shaping values, attitudes, and social norms. Teachers and administrators often serve as role models, and for some students, classrooms provide the sole source of diversity.

Curriculum choices also contribute to this socialization process, influencing not only what students learn about history, culture, and social structures but also their perspectives and points of view. For instance, during segregation, textbooks in southern US states often romanticized the institution of American slavery, presenting it in a misleading manner. Some educational materials minimized the violence and dehumanization of the enslaved, instead portraying enslavers as benevolent and paternalistic. Enslaved people were referred to as "workers" with little to no mention of the brutal physical punishment, sexual violence, and the denial of autonomy into which they were forced. Some curricula also framed slavery as an economic necessity rather than a moral atrocity.

While such narratives have faced widespread criticism and rejection as educators, historians, and activists work to present a more accurate and comprehensive history of slavery in the United States, the work remains far from over. Some school jurisdictions are moving these efforts backward based on the flawed argument that a more "balanced" approach is necessary to avoid making White students feel "uncomfortable." The curricula offered to students impact their lives in major ways, so when education excludes diverse perspectives or presents certain groups in negative and stereotypical ways, those teachings can negatively impact students' perceptions and attitudes.

Efforts to ban books that teach historical truths about nondominant cultures demonstrate the powerful impact of excluding different perspectives. Members of the dominant culture in America (White persons) are so afraid of what members of other cultures may think or do if permitted to learn these historical truths about how their cultures were and continue to be treated that they risk violating the First Amendment to the Constitution to be sure these truths cannot be read or talked about. In fact, between 2022 and 2024 alone, more than 400 bills spanning 42 states were introduced to attack DEI, to either restrict or regulate DEI initiatives over the concern that DEI fosters "White guilt."[1]

In 2024, the governor of Alabama, Kay Ivey, signed a bill that seeks to manipulate educational socialization by prohibiting divisive teachings around race, gender, or identity.[2] The legislation includes eight so-called "divisive concepts" relating to race, ethnicity, sex, religion, and national origin, banning any program that "advocates for a divisive concept," which, under some academic settings, includes references to slavery and the people who administered it.[3] In other words, it is more important that the White citizens of Alabama not feel badly or uncomfortable learning and talking about how their ancestors treated other cultures than to begin to heal the lingering wounds caused to those who have suffered unimaginable deaths and indignities for more than 400 years for no reason other than the color of their skin and/or who they love. It is clear that they are afraid of and in no way interested in the Truth—certainly not the whole truth. Their learned behaviors have made their comfort so important that laws are passed to protect it. Why? Because they feel guilty. They know wrong was done but are in no way interested in the discomfort of those continuing to suffer the legacy of the egregious wrongs perpetrated on their ancestors. They have been taught to operate from a place of terminal privilege at the cost of everyone who is not like them, underscoring the need for that which they seek to eliminate—education about DEI. Unfortunately, the current US administration is working to nationalize this same privileged line of thinking.

Media is a powerful tool for shaping learned behaviors and perceptions, with the representation (or lack thereof) of different groups in television and movies potentially reinforcing stereotypes and prejudices. The media has exposed generations of individuals to stereotypes based on gender, race, ethnicity, ability, and sexual orientation, and those portrayals have a societal impact as viewers internalize them and develop biased attitudes based on what they have seen or heard on television. Entertainment, for entertainment's sake, regardless of impact, can be dangerous.

In today's interconnected world, social media has profoundly influenced our societal dynamics. Generation Alpha—kids born between 2010 and 2024—is the first not to know a world without social media. The benefits of greater connectivity, information dissemination, and community building also have the paradoxical effect of fostering dangerous societal division. The ultimate goal of social media algorithms is to maximize user engagement, which is accomplished through echo chambers where users are primarily exposed to content and opinions that reinforce their existing beliefs and past social media behavior. Filters keep users from seeing diverse perspectives, reducing the opportunity for constructive dialogue and increasing the dangers of ideological polarization. As a result, individuals become more entrenched in their views and less open to communicating with people who hold alternative perspectives.

This type of siloed environment creates a fertile ground for the dissemination of misinformation to extremely large audiences. Generally crafted to evoke emotional responses, misinformation spreads more easily in homogenous spaces where it is less likely to be challenged. The individuals who frequent these social media spaces are more inclined to accept false information without scrutiny because it aligns with their preexisting beliefs. When only exposed to affirming viewpoints, people become increasingly confident in their perspectives, even if those views are based on incomplete or inaccurate information. This perspective erodes critical thinking skills and reduces the likelihood of constructive dialogue across differing ideologies.

The widespread acceptance and sharing of misinformation can lead to real-world consequences, including polarization, distrust in institutions, reinforcement of stereotypes, fear-mongering, and hatred. The anonymity of social media adds fuel to this conflict by offering a place where individuals feel emboldened to aggressively and inappropriately express even the most vial opinions. As a result, social media platforms have become notorious environments for harassment, bullying, and hate speech. Yes, extremist groups existed before social media, but these platforms have gone a long way in amplifying dangerous views that used to be marginalized, providing a broader audience to influence and a much easier tool for spreading divisive and dangerous content.

Social media has been an integral part of reinforcing group polarization and the practice of "othering." By only associating with like-minded individuals, people form tribal-type groups as they seek to distinguish themselves from out-groups, furthering a more divided society. Unfortunately, online communities and social media platforms have been instrumental in spreading and maintaining the vilest aspects of our society.

Influences like families, communities, educational institutions, traditional media, and social media significantly shape an individual's perspectives. From the foundational beliefs passed on by families to the societal biases often woven into the structure and curriculum of our educational institutions, young people are exposed to external messages that will impact them into their adult lives. Furthered by the unchecked privatization of traditional media and the siloed thinking of social media platforms, these learned behaviors, left unchecked, become the fabric of our society.

SOCIETY'S UNDERLYING THREAD OF WHITE SUPREMACY

The terms "White supremacy" and "White nationalism" have a lengthy history in the American lexicon. "White supremacy" was used as early as the mid-nineteenth century to describe the belief that the White race is inherently superior to all other races. The concept gained prominence as a justification for the historical enslavement of Black people. It was used as a groundwork for the laws and societal norms that upheld racial segregation and inequality.

The White supremacy ideology played a central role in the formation of the Ku Klux Klan, which was founded as a social club in Pulaski, Tennessee, in 1865 (not ironically, the same year in which the last enslaved people were informed they had been freed by the Emancipation Proclamation two years earlier).[4] Within two years, several more branches were formed, and their first organizing convention was held to create what they referred to as the "Invisible Empire of the South." To carry out their plans, members terrorized Black people throughout the southern states, along with anyone who attempted to help them. By 1870, there were KKK branches in nearly every southern state, manifesting in acts of extreme violence and intimidation well into the 1900s.

White supremacy has also shown up within our governmental policies. The Asian American Pacific Islander (AAPI) community faced one of the most blatant violations of civil rights during World War II. In response to the Pearl Harbor attacks, President Franklin D. Roosevelt signed an executive order directing that people of Japanese descent, including US citizens, be interned in prison camps and "relocation centers." Within hours of the bombing, FBI agents arrested more than one thousand Japanese Americans of all ages. Despite no evidence of wrongdoing, these people's lives were completely upended and their basic humanities disregarded.

Every person who was at least one-sixteenth Japanese was forcibly relocated, including seventeen thousand children, as well as several thousand elderly and disabled residents.[5] People were given mere days to dispose of their belongings before being forced to leave their homes and businesses unoccupied. They were placed in internment camps plagued with overcrowding, substandard sanitation, and food shortages. Though the US government closed the last Japanese internment camp in March 1946, it took another forty years for Congress to issue a formal apology and award reparations to over eighty thousand Japanese Americans.

In the early 1970s, the White supremacist movements and ideologies began to evolve into an ideological belief that White people should maintain a separate national identity and that their culture and interests should be preserved above those of other racial or ethnic groups. It was termed *White nationalism*, and it quickly gained a place in discussions surrounding race, identity, and US politics. According to the Southern Poverty Law Center, White nationalists focus on the alleged inferiority of non-White persons with the primary goal of creating a White ethnostate.[6] It also categorizes groups like neo-Nazis and racist skinheads as White nationalists.

While both of these concepts, *White supremacy* and *White nationalism*, have been around for generations, they have each gained new prominence in the public discourse over the last decade due in part to the widening gap in racial harmony that was witnessed during and since the initial presidency of Donald Trump. The political right has become entrenched in theories around the so-called "great replacement" of White people, driving strict opposition to immigration and a growing sentiment that national belonging should be determined by race. The attack on "wokeness," a term crafted within Black vernacular to denote awareness of social and racial injustices, has become the target of a racist backlash that has spilled over into attacks against DEI efforts.

These dangerous perspectives represent much more than simple differences in opinion or healthy political debate. They are steeped in White supremacist and White nationalist rhetoric and drive institutional policies that continuously undermine the justice and equality of our society. This thinking fosters intolerance and bigotry by creating an environment overflowing with fear and mistrust among different racial and ethnic groups. It tears at the fabric of a diverse and inclusive society by discouraging the multiculturalism and cooperation that are necessary for social harmony and progress.

In a society that upholds democratic values, White nationalism is fundamentally at odds with the principles that keep our democracy in place. It undermines the democratic process, erodes our civil liberties, and weakens our democratic institutions by encouraging exclusionary and authoritarian views.

A SOCIETY BUILT ON PATRIARCHY

Patriarchy is a male-dominated social system perpetuated through various forms of socialization and institutional reinforcement where men hold the overwhelming majority of power and women are largely denied it. American society is deeply entrenched in patriarchal structures. From antiquated laws to the pervasive gender pay gap (another tortuous reality that makes absolutely no sense), patriarchy has fostered an environment where gender-based exploitation is normalized and systemic. Our country's history is marked by persistent inequalities even despite the significant strides toward gender equality. Yes, progress has been made, but the pervasiveness of patriarchy is still very present, evidenced by the consistent dehumanizing of women and girls.

A pervasive issue throughout American history, gender discrimination has resulted in barriers to education, employment, and political power for women. This started with British law, which gave husbands control over property their wives brought into the marriage and extended into the American colonies, which followed suit with similar stipulations. In 1771, New York became the first US state to grant women limited property rights, giving them some say in managing assets jointly owned with their husbands.[7] In 1787, Massachusetts changed its law to allow married women of European descent to run the family business in their husbands' absence.[8] Women of African descent and Native American women were excluded.

The widespread failure to recognize the humanity of women extended to more than property. Generations of women took on the suffrage movement, fighting for their right to participate in the American political process. At the historical 1848 Seneca Falls Convention, women abolitionists demanded their right to vote while also delivering their Declaration of Sentiments, which stated, "We hold these truths to be self-evident; that all men and women are created equal."[9] The right to vote was finally granted to women in 1920 with the ratification of the Nineteenth Amendment to the US Constitution. However, many women of color were disallowed to exercise that right until decades later.

These misogynistic, patriarchal attitudes have impacted virtually every aspect of women's lives throughout the history of America, including their inclusion within the workplace. In the early 1900s, most working women did so within very specific segments of the workforce that had been deemed "women's" jobs, such as teachers, nurses, or housekeepers. However, that changed drastically during World War II when women were called upon to work the jobs left behind by men serving in the military.

Millions of women went to work in factories and shipyards nationwide. They built military warships, planes, munitions, and supplies. These women were invaluable to the war effort and maintaining the American economy during the war. Yet, when the war ended, so did their jobs. Women were forced to leave the workplace and expected to return to their former jobs as men returned from war and went back into the factories for work.

As growing numbers of college-educated women entered the corporate world, the 1960s brought about major changes for women in the workplace. At the same time, the growing feminist movement was calling attention to issues like pay disparity, hiring discrimination, and unchecked sexual harassment in the workplace. Women demanded workplace changes from their political representatives and the courts. The Equal Pay Act of 1963 resulted from those efforts as the first US legislation to "prohibit discrimination on account of sex in the payment of wages by employers engaged in commerce or in the production of goods for commerce."[10] Yet, sixty years later, the pay disparities between men and women remain a stark reminder that women still fight for their humanity.

The historical perception of women as property to be bought and sold has also fostered an environment for sexual exploitation to thrive. When gender equality is limited, so is access to education and economic opportunities. The result is an economic disparity that makes women and girls more vulnerable to the traffickers who prey on their needs and lure them with promises of financial stability and better living conditions. It is a devaluation that makes our society ripe for the dangers of sex trafficking, an ever-growing problem that has taken hold in today's society.

These economic factors are exemplified in the populations with the highest risk of trafficking. Regardless of gender, homeless youth and runaways, undocumented immigrants, and members of the LGBTQ+ community are all disproportionately affected, primarily due to the lack of support systems, family rejection, and the societal discrimination that these groups face. They are stereotyped as weaker and less than in a patriarchal society, which makes them easy targets for traffickers who exploit their need for acceptance and safety.

Further complicating matters, the patriarchy places a stigma of shame around sexual exploitation, which discourages victims from reporting their crimes. The inherent power imbalance empowers traffickers to manipulate and control with impunity. Victims don't speak out for fear of facing discrimination, shame, and ostracization, only compounding their trauma. In many regions of the US, legal and societal discrimination against LGBTQ+ individuals compounds the problem of trafficking. Laws that criminalize same-sex relationships or non-binary gender identities can prevent victims from seeking help or reporting abuse. Fear of arrest or further victimization by authorities can keep LGBTQ+ trafficking victims from accessing the justice and protection they deserve.

At its core, sex trafficking exploits individuals, predominantly women and children, for commercial sexual mistreatment. This exploitation not only violates fundamental human rights but also undermines the fabric of our society by perpetuating cycles of violence, trauma, and injustice. It reinforces harmful stereotypes and social exclusion, causing a ripple effect that contributes to higher rates of mental health issues, substance abuse, and other social problems within the community. The internet and social media have played a significant role in evolving the sex trafficking industry. Traffickers can now use online platforms to recruit, advertise, and exploit their victims, often under the guise of legitimate work opportunities. They can operate with a degree of anonymity and reach a larger pool of potential victims and buyers, making it harder for law enforcement to track and combat these activities.

Patriarchy lies at the center of many of our societal breakdowns. It consistently perpetuates the misconception of gender inequality between men and women while also contributing to the sexual violence that plagues people of all genders and sexual orientations. As men, and White men in particular, continue to benefit from patriarchy, its detrimental effects on women and other underrepresented groups persist.

SHEDDING LIGHT ON THE TRUTH

The summer of 2020 was a profound moment in history, a time when America's deep-seated issues of systematic oppression took center stage on a global platform. The tragic and senseless murder of George Floyd by a police officer in Minneapolis ignited a worldwide movement. It became the catalyst for confronting the severe inequities and injustices faced by Black Americans and other marginalized communities every day.

For many, it was an eye-opening moment, revealing the extent to which oppression has been built into the fabric of our country and its societal ills, from policing and housing to healthcare, education, and employment. Unawareness could no longer be used as an excuse for indifference to the status quo that benefits some while it disadvantages others. Protests erupted around the world, creating a renewed focus on the need for substantial reforms and the dismantling of societal systems that perpetuate racial disparities, uphold privilege, and allow for bias against vulnerable communities.

The summer of 2020 held a mirror up to our society, spotlighting some ugly truths and demanding us to consider the need for reconciliation. Truths about the ideologies of White supremacy and male patriarchy that have historically driven so many systemic injustices. Truths about the power and influence of social media to drive change or exacerbate harm. The harsh light of day was shed on the truth, and the majority now seeks to push the truth back into darkness—to hide it, bury it, silence it. To what end? The truth is that the world is changing in significant ways, whether our White brethren like it or not. By 2044, the US population will likely be a majority-minority—not because of the "replacement theory" but because of demographic evolution.[11] What then?

True reconciliation requires that we are willing to face and embrace the real truths about our society so we can heal and move on. This requires that we question rather than mindlessly accept and that we set aside our biases to open our hearts and minds to explore perspectives different from our own. Doing so may illuminate the real truths about who and where we are as a society.

CHAPTER FOUR

The Truth About Acknowledgment and Forgiveness

Now that we've discussed the painful truths beneath our historical injustices and societal inequities, I want to change gears into a conversation about DEI, specifically, the roles that acknowledgment and forgiveness play in pursuing reconciliation. When we talk about forgiveness in the DEI space, most people automatically assume the conversation will center on groups that have been harmed or negatively impacted in some way. While this is, without doubt, an essential part of the discussion, it is not the focus of this chapter.

Instead, I want to discuss the forgiveness that we must provide ourselves. As we reflect on how we show up in the world, we start to recognize our own biases because we all have them. I know you may feel uncomfortable with that reality, and your initial response may even be denial, but the truth is that we all have biases. Period.

Reconciliation comes from acknowledging our biases, forgiving ourselves for where we find ourselves (which means releasing guilt and shame for our biases), and doing the work to ensure that our biases are not negatively impacting anyone else.

I start each DEI presentation with a few nonnegotiable guidelines. First, TRUTH trainings are judgment-free zones, where all questions are good questions and all opinions and perspectives are respected. Second, the trainings provide a brave space where we acknowledge that pushing ourselves leads to growth, and as such, it is okay to be uncomfortable.

The purpose of these guidelines is to help people relax and lean into the process. A lot of anxiety exists around DEI, especially among White males. They often come into the training space with negativity, expecting that they will be made to feel guilty and shameful. Instead, the TRUTH trainings aim to help trainees not feel guilt or shame, as they are neither necessary nor productive and can hinder your ability to move forward. TRUTH trainings invite you to move past those feelings, push them away, and replace them with forgiveness.

ACKNOWLEDGMENT

There can be no reconciliation without acknowledgment; for me, a big part of acknowledgment is being authentic and vulnerable. The painful truth is that we all have played a part in creating or upholding systemic inequities, whether directly or indirectly, and I am no exception.

In 2005, I leaped at the opportunity to start a legal department with the Diamondbacks organization. I had never done anything like that before, and I was uncertain about taking on such a big responsibility, but I did not let that stop me. What started as a department of one grew to three attorneys, a paralegal, and an executive assistant, a pretty good size for an in-house professional sports team legal department.

In 2020, following the murder of George Floyd, the president and CEO of the Diamondbacks decided he wanted to do something very intentional with respect to diversity. We started the D-backs for Change Justice, Equity, Diversity, and Inclusion (JEDI) Council, and I asked to lead the council. I was among very few women or people of color on the broader leadership team. I was the only woman, the only person of color, and the only gay person at the executive leadership level of the organization. I thought there was no one better suited to lead the organization's DEI efforts than me.

I knew that I could pull from my decades of lived experience as an openly gay Black woman of a certain age. Still, I also thought it was important to acquire DEI credentials to go along with it. I entered the Cornell DEI Certification Program and earned my DEI certification. During this time, I learned of Harvard University's Implicit Association Test (IAT), a tool that the university created to help people identify their own implicit biases and understand the effect that those biases may have on their beliefs, actions, and treatment of others. From my training and personal observations, I knew I had some personal biases. Still, I took the test anyway because I was not as sure about what those biases were. To my surprise, the results stated that I was biased toward people with lighter complexions, a revelation that left me both surprised and ashamed.

I pondered that bias a lot, realizing that it may have been attributed to my own internalized racism and that it could also have been about where I was in my life. At the time, I was working in professional sports with limited diversity at the executive and leadership levels. My immediate peers on the executive leadership team were all White men, and I wondered how much of my bias stemmed from my loyalty to the organization and the economic success it afforded to me. I could have stayed stuck in that reality and beat myself up for not showing up in the world in the way that I thought I was. But instead, I decided to acknowledge my bias, forgive myself for having it, and do the work of managing and, ultimately, eliminating my bias.

Leading the JEDI council, along with my duties as executive vice president and chief legal officer, was a labor of love that eventually began to take a toll on my health and made me question what I was doing. After a series of life-threatening illnesses and injuries, it became clear that I couldn't continue to carry that heavy load. I gave a lot of thought to what I should do and what I wanted to do. I contemplated giving up the DEI work and just focusing on my legal work, but I knew in my heart I would not be able to step back from it. Ultimately, I decided that if I had to choose between my legal work and the DEI work I felt called to do at that time, I would choose DEI. I strongly believed that it was my purpose at that time in my life and that by doing it, I could make a difference in the world. I absolutely loved my years working in professional sports and with the Diamondbacks. It was my dream job and my work home, and I will be forever grateful for it all. But as we grow, our priorities change. And for me, doing DEI work and doing my part to improve this world was my priority.

After working for some time in the DEI space, I retook the Harvard IAT test and found that my bias had changed in favor of darker-skinned people, which made sense in a way because my surroundings and focus in life were very different. My unconscious bias had become very conscious, given my focus on helping people who are historically underserved and marginalized obtain equity and get to a place of true equality. The test showed me how our biases can sometimes reflect our circumstances if we don't live in a place of awareness. I reconciled that I have a bias, and I continue to make a very conscious effort to ensure that everyone I work with—no matter who they are—understands that they have some dimension(s) of diversity and that we all have a place in this conversation and in the work towards inclusive communities and workplaces.

Reconciliation demands an honest reckoning with the truth about ourselves, our organizations, and society, and none of us should seek to run away or hide from those truths for a few very compelling reasons. First, many of us do not have the privilege or luxury of running away. Our daily realities provide a constant reminder that biases and injustices exist. Whether it's a microaggression from a coworker or a blatant demonstration of bias in the grocery store, these experiences demand a heightened awareness of the inequities around us, making it virtually impossible for a vast segment of the population to run and hide.

Second, facing the uncomfortable truth about your biases is a moral imperative and a necessary step toward justice. Our acknowledgment—reconciling our truth—helps us face the past with clarity and humility so we can better understand how privilege and oppression have shaped our workplaces and societal structures. It validates the existence of deep inequities so that steps can be taken to dismantle them.

Finally, if you are a person who can run and hide or ignore the inequities faced by others around you, ask yourself why. What are you afraid to learn about yourself? Is it the hurt of recognizing the inconsistencies between who you want to be and how you actually show up in the world? If you are a person who simply does not care about systemic injustices, then ask yourself why you don't care. Is it because you don't feel the effects of inequity in your life? Are you so comfortable with your position within these systems that you don't recognize the people who have been locked out? Are you choosing a lack of awareness over empathy? We can't chart a path for where we need to go if we don't acknowledge where we are.

UNSTUCKNESS

Once you acknowledge your personal biases, your next question will hopefully be, "How do I move forward and do better from here?" For some people, the next question may be, "How did I get here," which is also acceptable, especially if the answer helps to get you unstuck from the guilt. However, the most crucial step in moving forward toward reconciliation is forgiveness.

Deedra Determan is the founder of D2 Branding, an author, and my business coach. In our work together, she shared insights into her acknowledgment journey and the forgiveness that followed.

"Obviously, I knew that racism was out there, but I definitely lived in a bubble. I had been a little naïve, and hearing Nona's story just opened my eyes. She is a successful Black woman in Major League Baseball leadership. 'Who's discriminating against her?' I thought because she was in a really high-profile job, making the money, and doing the thing, she had somehow transcended that type of treatment. But I learned that none of her accomplishments could stop her from being followed around a store by a clerk, thinking that she's going to take something. Learning what she went through and seeing it in her eyes really made a difference for me."

As Deedra became increasingly aware of the biases that impact people who look and love like me, she began to feel some of that guilt and shame. "One of the first things Nona told me was to not feel guilty," Deedra said. "But it just felt so hard because I haven't had to deal with anything like that in my life. With everything in life, nobody needs this extra unneeded stress. There are enough stressful things in the world."

Forgiveness in the context of this chapter should serve as a catalyst for action, not an endpoint or a hall pass to sit idly by on the DEI sidelines. It's about transforming guilt and shame into unstuckness and contributing to a more equitable future, not dismissing or excusing historical injustices. Nor is it about absolving oneself of any current privilege or complicity in systemic inequities. Forgiveness can be problematic without accountability, and it becomes easy to minimize or completely ignore the ongoing harm caused by bias and inequalities.

GETTING TO RECONCILIATION

I hope we will all be able to eliminate our biases at some point, but until then, it's important for us all to be aware of what they are so we can manage them. Reconciliation comes once you know where you are and find a way to forgive yourself so you can move forward. Owning and understanding it is part of the human experience, but commit to doing better and take action to actually do better.

When we look at Germany, we want them to be honest about what happened with the Nazis and Hitler's reign. And when we look at South Africa and apartheid, we want them to be honest about what happened there and their constitution. Yet, we struggle to be honest about our history in the United States. And as long as we continuously turn away from acknowledgment and forgiveness, we will never truly get there. You can have a heart of gold, but if you don't fully understand the problem you're trying to fix, you will often come up with solutions that, at best, maintain the status quo and, at worst, uphold false narratives that distort history.

Reconciliation is not about running and hiding. As difficult as it may be, it's about embracing that truth completely and forgiving yourself for it. Understanding that your willingness to look at it and acknowledge it is a reason for you not to feel guilt or shame. You are accepting where you are and not beating yourself up for it. Because if you can accept it and forgive yourself, there's no reason to be stuck in guilt or shame or hide from the work. It's going through that process of saying, okay, this is where you are, but you can't stay stuck here because you're too ashamed to talk about it or too afraid to confront it or face it or acknowledge that it's where you are, that you can't move forward.

Understanding

CHAPTER FIVE

The Truth About the Disruptors of DEI—Bias

So far, in our exploration of TRUTH, we have talked about embracing what Truth is and Reconciling the truth to get to a place of Understanding. A large part of understanding is recognizing the actions and mindsets that seek to interrupt the natural order of DEI that should exist within our workplaces and society. Diversity is already here, and equity and inclusion would follow if we all acted with respect for one another's humanity. Yet, the biases that we carry around have disrupted the equity and inclusion that would otherwise exist. In this chapter, we'll discuss three common types of bias: group bias, conscious bias, and unconscious bias. These primary disruptors are often built deep inside the policies, practices, and systems, ensuring that workplaces feel unsafe and unwelcoming.

GROUP BIAS

In June of 2023, a group of friends stopped at a New York gas station to fill up their tank. While waiting, they decided to have some harmless fun and vogue, an improvisational dance style popularized by the LGBTQ+ community. As they danced and enjoyed themselves, a group of men approached them, using homophobic and racist slurs, demanding that they stop and inciting a confrontation. In the end, the life of a twenty-eight-year-old Black gay man was taken violently. O'Shae Sibley was a beloved professional dancer and choreographer who lost his life due to the senseless hatred and bias of a group of people.

Bias is an opinion, feeling, or influence that strongly favors one side in an argument or one item in a group or series. It is a preconceived opinion or attitude about people with shared physical characteristics or cultural experiences. Biases may be conscious or unconscious and can show up in various forms. They create false assumptions, but one way to overcome those assumptions is to focus on the truth.

Group bias refers to the tendency for people to show favoritism toward others within their group and unfairness towards people who are not members of their group. It stems from the human tendency to experience the world around us through our lens of "us" and "them." We take part in this categorization as a mechanism for navigating the world around us. We operate under the belief that if we can assign people to specific categories and groups, we can better understand them based on the characterizations we associate with members of that group.

Our need for social identity also drives group biases. Our association with specific social groups can make us feel better about ourselves, which in turn contributes to our level of self-esteem. That desire to see ourselves positively drives the desire also to see members of our group positively and, conversely, members of other groups negatively. Researchers have linked these feelings to the survival instincts of our ancestors, who needed to work in small groups in order to secure the resources they needed to survive. Supporting your group, even to the detriment of another group, meant fighting for your survival. As a result, members of other groups were seen as enemies and potential impediments to our well-being. This type of thinking has been ingrained in our minds for generations—to the point where we rarely even recognize our group biases unless they are pointed out or we intentionally try to identify them.

Group bias is the type of bias that resulted in the death of that young man for doing nothing more than dancing and living in his truth. It is the type of hatred that has fueled violent supremacy groups for generations. The Southern Poverty Law Center (SPLC) defines a hate group as "an organization that—based on its official statements or principles, the statements of its leaders, or its activities—has beliefs or practices that attack or malign an entire class of people, typically for their immutable characteristics." In 2020, SPLC listed 940 active hate groups across the country. These organizations demonstrate violent biases towards others based on race, religion, ethnicity, sexual orientation, or gender identity.

However, group bias does not have to rise to the level of violence to be consequential. When we treat people outside of our groups unfairly, it can lead to stereotypical thinking based on the belief that all group members carry the same characteristics. It's a "They're all the same" mentality that exaggerates group members' similarities. The creation of double standards is another danger of group bias. We may scoff at other groups' behaviors or characteristics while tolerating and celebrating the same behaviors amongst our group. We see this all the time within the political realm of a system dominated by two political parties. The disdain or glorification of a politician's actions often depends on whether they share our political affiliation.

When we get wrapped up in group bias, we risk missing out on impactful relationships with members of other groups. We may limit contact with people of different races, backgrounds, or educational levels. We may also blame and scapegoat these groups' members to protect ourselves and our groups. The blame placed on immigrants is an example. Even when in the United States legally, many immigrants find themselves on the receiving end of undeserved blame for one or more societal problems.

CONSCIOUS BIAS

Conscious bias, sometimes called explicit bias, is the type of bias a person is aware of. They knowingly and intentionally act with a bias towards someone. These behaviors process at a conscious level and may come out in a variety of ways, including physical abuse, verbal harassment, or exclusionary actions. An injured person who refuses to be treated by anyone other than a White male doctor is exhibiting a conscious bias.

My childhood experience with the KKK provided my first introduction to conscious (and group) bias. Members of this hate group are American White supremacists who employ terror against others outside of their group based on their shared belief that anyone outside of their race and beliefs is inferior. They knowingly belong to this organization and have a vast history of intentionally employing tactics to intimidate and terrorize others.

UNCONSCIOUS BIAS

Opposite conscious bias lies unconscious bias, a disruptor even more dangerous because we often don't know that we have it and are unaware of its impact on the people around us. Every single second, we each receive eleven million bits of information through our combined five senses. Our nervous system serves as a channel for transmitting it all, with the brain acting as a processing and messaging center. Yet, our brains can only process forty bits of information per second, which leaves 99.999996 percent of received information to be processed unconsciously.

Our brain draws upon our preexisting knowledge structures and prior experiences to create shortcuts, which leads to unconscious biases. We all have human brains, so we all have unconscious biases. They are a product of our lived experiences, including our families, our education, where we grew up, the movies we watch, and countless other factors. We fall short of overcoming these biases because we don't explore these assumptions on our own, instead choosing to accept them as true.

There are many types of unconscious bias, but herein, we will focus on five specific types.

Attributing Value Bias

Attributing value bias is the attribution of certain qualities to a person or thing based on our initial perceived values about them. These beliefs are not based on actual values or any tangible information. Yet, they lead us to impute superior value or quality to something or someone that we find more appealing or esteemed. For instance, a person may attribute traits like intelligence, skill, or honesty to people they find physically attractive, even without knowing anything about their personality or integrity.

The attributing value bias can also work in the opposite direction, leading us to ignore or disregard people and things that do not jump out as immediately attractive in some way. We often see this in the workplace, where leaders and managers make decisions based on their attributing value biases.

Numerous studies have been conducted regarding hiring decisions and the treatment of applicants solely based on the ethnicity of names. For example, research has shown that while one out of ten applicants with White-sounding names received a callback, only one out of fifteen applicants with Black-sounding names received a callback. In other words, Black applicants received fifty percent fewer callbacks.[1]

An abundance of research also exists around attributing value bias within the realm of workplace performance reviews. Managers may give more consideration to the value of work done by their favorite employees while undervaluing less favored employees. This may also show up as a supervisor undeservedly attributing successes or misses to employees instead of to the external factors that actually cause them.

Leadership decisions can also be impacted by attributing value biases. Positions of authority may be given out based on physical attributes, such as skin color or gender, rather than basing such decisions on capabilities, experience, and a successful track record. This can also be seen in business meetings, where the contributions of women are ignored while the same contributions are embraced when offered by male employees. People often attribute more value to the ideas of men in the workplace, a bias that frequently leads to a gender imbalance in leadership hierarchies.

Another common attributing value bias within the professional workplace is the preference for applicants from "prestigious" universities. The perceived value of these institutions is automatically attributed to the applicant, such that many large law firms will not consider hiring lawyer applicants who did not attend top-tier law schools.

My decision to attend law school came at the very last minute. I chose Oklahoma City University School of Law solely based on the fact that their application period was still open. Within three weeks, I got accepted, moved all my belongings to Oklahoma City, and started law school. I attended a "minority" job fair in Dallas while still in law school. Among other firms in Dallas and Phoenix, I landed an interview with a big law firm in New York. I was excited to meet with them and filled with optimism about where it could lead for my career. However, upon meeting with them, I was told they wanted to meet me because they were impressed with my résumé but would never hire me because I went to Oklahoma City

University instead of a top-tier law school. To this day, I do not understand why they wasted my time.

This is the type of systematic bias that keeps many capable and highly skilled applicants from professional opportunities, and it typically impacts people from marginalized and historically underrepresented groups who are often more than qualified for the position.

Assumptions about résumé gaps are another way that attributing value bias shows up. There are numerous reasons why a job applicant may have gaps in their work history. They may have been caring for a child or an elderly family member. Perhaps they traveled the world for a year, learning new languages and experiencing new cultures. That gap may even represent a return to school for additional training, or maybe it was a necessary mental health break. While none of these circumstances makes an applicant unprofessional or unemployable, many employers view résumé gaps through that narrow lens.

Without even asking for more details, they instinctively disregard the résumé, which can negatively affect the diversity of the applicant pool. Women are overwhelmingly more likely to interrupt their career journeys, particularly when needing to care for family members. As such, when employers instantly reject résumés with gaps, they are quite possibly rejecting some very capable women candidates.

Yet another way that attributing value bias shows up in the workplace is when employers require degrees that are not needed for the position. Over the last ten years, a growing number of employers have made bachelor's degrees a requirement for new workers in positions that traditionally have not required that level of formal education. This trend, often called "degree inflation," is typically based on the belief that college-educated applicants bring more productivity and engagement to these jobs than those without a degree. However, these assumptions purposely ignore a large segment of highly capable candidates who may not have had the opportunity or means to attend college. Further complicating this attributing value bias issue is the fact that many of these employers utilize automated technologies during the hiring process. These tools ensure that candidates without college degrees never even have an opportunity to complete the application process, let alone to interview for a position for which they are completely qualified.

Attributing value bias can be addressed with a variety of strategies:

- Seek out and receive input from others different from you. If you are making a hiring or promotion decision and want to ensure your decision is fair and does not involve attributing value bias, double-check your decision with someone different from you. Checking in with someone who brings a different lens to the conversation is helpful but only if you are willing to consider their perspective.
- Implement a diverse hiring committee. Bringing numerous diverse perspectives into the process helps ensure that all applicants for a position or a promotion receive fair and equitable consideration.
- Implement a blind résumé process for hiring where personal candidate details like name, gender, age, and contact

information are omitted. Anonymize or exclude any educational institutions that may be associated with socioeconomic status or geographical bias. Education- and employment history-related data can also be removed to prevent age bias.

Affinity Bias

Affinity bias describes our tendency to favor people with interests, backgrounds, and experiences similar to our own. We all tend to feel more comfortable around people like us, which is not a problem within our personal relationships. However, this tendency can also cause us to rebuff people who do not share our interests, which can create significant problems if left unchecked, particularly within the workplace. Affinity bias is a shortcut for trust through the gravitation towards people you like and with whom you have something in common.

Affinity bias can show up in the workplace in a couple of ways. First, it can manifest through the interview process, where hiring partners may make decisions based on commonalities with job applicants. For instance, a hiring manager may hire a fellow sorority member over another, more experienced candidate who does not share that commonality. It can also show up in job assignments, where a supervisor may give the best job assignments or most favorable work schedule to a subordinate with whom they share a love of pickleball, which they frequently discuss at the office.

The best way to address affinity bias is to check yourself! Be intentional about treating everyone fairly. If you find that you are hiring someone you really like and have something in common with over other very qualified candidates, interrogate yourself to be sure bias hasn't crept in. If it has, reevaluate your decision and be sure you're being fair and hiring the best person for the job.

Systemic Bias

Systemic bias, sometimes called *institutional bias*, is prejudice, discrimination, and unfairness in policies and practices that have the effect of creating advantages for those from advantaged groups and oppression and disadvantage for those from groups classified as marginalized or underrepresented. We discussed systems of oppression in great detail in chapter 3, but it is important to note that these structured biases consistently show up within the workplace, including the following circumstances:

- Discriminatory hiring and promotion patterns
- Segregated work environments
- Marginalization or exclusion from group activities, like team-building events

Assessment reviews are extremely valuable for addressing systematic bias. All institutions and organizations must be examined for these invisible, often unconscious policies, customs, language, practices, and economic structures that give some people an unfair advantage over others, and they must eliminate these structures to eliminate systematic bias.

Confirmation Bias

Confirmation bias is the tendency to favor information that confirms your beliefs. You assume your thoughts and opinions are correct, regardless of the facts. This type of bias keeps us from objectively analyzing situations, which can lead to poor choices. For instance, once a manager has labeled someone as a lazy employee with no justification, they may view everything that employee does as being lethargic. Even if that person is dealing with a medical problem or being impacted by external workplace factors, their lack of success is attributed to laziness.

Women and parents may deal with confirmation biases in many ways within the workplace. A working parent who occasionally needs to work from home while dealing with childcare may be seen as not hardworking or lacking in dedication to their professional journey. A pregnant woman may be looked over for a promotion based on the assumption that she is more invested in growing her family and no longer interested in climbing the leadership ladder.

To address confirmation bias, start taking a genuine interest in different perspectives. Be diligent about seeking out all available information, not just the information that confirms your existing views. To combat confirmation bias, we must be open to changing our minds.

Proximity Bias

Proximity bias involves the instinctual preference for people close to us in physical proximity. It is an unconscious bias favoring what or whom we see regularly. Though not new, proximity bias has become prevalent with the shift to remote work brought on by the pandemic. Leaders, sometimes influenced by resentment of those working remotely, tend to view employees in close proximity as more devoted, while remote workers are regarded with an "out of sight, out of mind" mentality. Managers with a proximity bias may make remote employees feel like their career trajectory lags, and there may be some truth to that. Within the typical work environment, not being present for office get-togethers and informal conversations can cause a great disadvantage when it comes to evaluations and leadership opportunities. These workers are left out of important discussions, which may leave them with limited opportunities for advancement.

What are some strategies for minimizing proximity bias? First, executive leaders in an organization must be made aware of proximity bias so managers displaying the bias can be coached through it and corrected. Research has shown that developing a writing-based culture—where all information is written and shared on a central platform where it is available to everyone—is also effective.

THE IMPACT OF UNCONSCIOUS BIAS

Unconscious bias can have a significant impact on our personal and professional lives. It can influence our decisions, such as what we purchase and from whom we purchase. It can impact our relationships—who we have them with, who we share information with, and who we choose to spend time with. In the workplace, it can impact who we choose to do business with, who we hire and promote, to whom we give feedback and who we are comfortable receiving it from, and to whom we give the best work assignments. These impacts are costly as they exclude, albeit unconsciously, very qualified and deserving people who have done nothing to deserve it.

Managing unconscious bias begins with the mindset because how you think and what you internalize can often drive how you behave. We must start by recognizing that (1) we are human, and because we are human, we all have unconscious biases, and (2) having unconscious biases does not make us bad people. Instead of feeling guilty about having a bias, look for an opportunity to do something different.

After recognizing the bias, the next step in managing unconscious bias is identifying its negative impacts so we can address our biases in real-time. A bias that negatively impacts others can be incredibly dangerous to our growth and the growth of those around us, so it's essential to consider all viewpoints to get an appropriate perspective and manage our biases. When we do this, we demonstrate authenticity and vulnerability and can become a model for others for how to own our biases, work on them, and change our behavior.

Implementing DEI programs within an organization requires identifying what bias exists, where it exists, and how to eliminate it. For example, what are the diversity numbers within hiring practices, promotions, and pay increases? Those metrics don't lie, and by monitoring them, leaders better understand how unconscious bias is showing up within the organization, which then provides an opportunity for mitigation.

MANAGING DISRUPTION

Merriam-Webster defines *disruption* as a break or interruption in the normal course or continuation of an activity or process. In other words, it is a break in the norm. As DEI efforts have been ongoing for the past few years and efforts are made to build more inclusive communities and workplaces, there has been an undercurrent of behaviors designed to disrupt progress.

We must also be open to allowing people to enhance our understanding, which is a hallmark of real leadership maturity. Employees appreciate leaders who share their viewpoints but also value the views of others. It also helps to remember that a commitment to the best outcome is more important than standing by a strong opinion. If we are committed to doing the work, we can take it a step further to become a change agent who also discusses the impacts of bias, provides solutions for our biases, and helps others with theirs.

CHAPTER SIX

The Truth About the Disruptors of DEI— Microaggressions and Privilege

Microaggressions and privilege undermine the values of respect, empathy, and equality that DEI upholds. Both the subtle dismissiveness of microaggressions and the unearned advantages of privilege corrode workplace culture by diminishing any sense of belonging and perpetuating systemic structures that favor inequities. These disruptors of DEI manifest in policies and practices that restrict opportunities, creating obstacles to diverse and inclusive environments.

MICROAGGRESSIONS

"No, but where are you really from?" Have you been asked this question because of the way you look or because you have an accent? As harmless as the questioner thinks this quest is to satisfy their curiosity, it is a hurtful and thoughtless microaggression. Microaggression is a comment or action that negatively targets a marginalized person or group. It may demean a person's race, gender, sexual orientation, age, or health status. Microaggressions often come in jokes, exclusion of voices in meetings, or subtle remarks that denigrate the recipient. They can be intentional, accidental, verbal, behavioral, or environmental. However, whatever form they take, microaggression is a serious form of discrimination. People who engage in them may mean no harm to the targeted person or group and may not even recognize that they are making a microaggression, but these words and actions are still hurtful. It is like death by a thousand cuts.

Here are some examples of microaggressions:

- Making assumptions about someone based on their race, religion, age, or class
- Complimenting someone raised in the United States on their English-speaking skills because they are not White
- Interrupting a woman when she is speaking
- Being unwilling to find stereotypical or derogatory sports teams' names offensive
- Using offensive terminology, such as "That's so gay."
- Gaslighting or telling someone they are being overly sensitive or that what they experienced is not evidence of bias. (I have

had this done to me a million times as a woman working in professional sports.)
- A waiter ignoring a person of color and waiting on a White person first
- College campuses naming buildings only after White people

A disparity exists between how people think they treat people from underrepresented communities and the harms that they are actually causing. So-called "harmless comments" have a significant effect, both within the workplace and in the personal lives of those who experience them, especially when they occur repeatedly. People of color often experience microaggressions aimed at their professional competencies, slights that have become common in the narrative against DEI, where highly skilled and education professionals are labeled DEI hires.

Women often experience microaggressions in the workplace as well. Women are often made responsible for office "housekeeping" duties. We must deal with the patronizing microaggression of "mansplaining," and we are told to "calm down" upon exhibiting any act of assertiveness. Women get overlooked for promotions based on assumptions about their ability to handle leadership stresses. When we speak up to defend ourselves, we may be met with additional microaggressions, like being ignored or labeled overly emotional.

ADDRESSING MICROAGGRESSIONS

The steps for responding to microaggressions vary depending on whether you have committed one, been the recipient, or witnessed one used against someone else. If you commit a microaggression and someone brings it to your attention, don't get defensive or be dismissive and turn into the poor, misunderstood victim; doing so is essentially committing another microaggression. Instead, listen to the recipient and empathize with their feelings. Take responsibility for the underlying bias that led to your actions and take steps to educate yourself with a greater sense of understanding. Commit to changing your micro-aggressive behaviors.

If you are the recipient of microaggression, respond to it in the moment only if it feels safe to do so. Sometimes, a microaggression is so offensive, insulting, or hurtful that the situation is not suitable for an immediate response. When you do speak to the person about it, let them know how it made you feel and why it is significant, but be sure to criticize the behavior and not the person. Criticizing the person will likely only make them defensive, which will not result in a productive conversation. It's also important to take care of yourself by seeking support from others by talking to them about what happened or by practicing some other form of self-care (such as going for a walk, meditating, or journaling).

If you witness microaggression, speak up! Bystander intervention can be key to nipping micro-aggressive behavior in the bud. For example, if a man interrupts or talks over a woman in a meeting, interrupt the interrupter so the woman can finish her statement. Highlight her accomplishments if others try to incorrectly diminish her abilities. When you speak up, however, it's important that you speak on your behalf rather than on behalf of the recipient of the microaggression. In other words, make it clear that the microaggression made you uncomfortable as a witness and explain why.

Finally, it's tremendously important and helpful to reach out to the recipient of a microaggression (whether you speak up or not) to validate their experience. Let them know that, as an ally, you recognize and understand what happened to them.

PRIVILEGE

Dr. Peggy McIntosh is a senior research scientist at the Wellesley Centers for Women. She directs the Gender, Race, and Inclusive Education Project, a program that facilitates workshops on privilege systems and diversifying workplaces. She defines privilege as "an invisible package of unearned assets which one can count on cashing in each and every day, but about which one is completely oblivious."[1] In other words, there are some things that some of us will never have to worry about or experience because of who we are. Our privileges give us advantages over others who do not share our privileges, making it a potent disruptor of DEI.

There are two types of privilege—unearned and earned—and we all have both types. Unearned privilege is not based on anything that we have done. We didn't put in any hard work or extra effort to get them. They are solely based on who we happen to be and the social groups to which we belong. It has to do with how we were born into the world and where our status lies. Things such as race, class, gender, and marital status are examples of unearned privilege. These unearned privileges appear in various ways that we may not consider. Being tall is an unearned privilege. Being right-handed is a privilege in a world built primarily for right-handed people. Being born male comes with certain privileges not available to females. And, in many countries, being born White comes with privileges not available to people of color. Being able-bodied certainly provides privileges not available to individuals who are disabled. And the list goes on. If you have never been asked where you are from or where you are "really" from, or if you've never had to worry about being harmed because of your gender identity, you are privileged.

Unlike unearned privileges, earned privileges are benefits based on your hard work and how you show up in the world. How do you respect others? Are you honest and courageous? Are you a good leader? Earned privilege accrues regardless of race, class, gender, or sexual orientation. Your college degree and advanced degrees, your hard-earned promotion, your championship trophy are examples of privileges that you've worked hard to earn.

Even a White person's last name can be an example of privilege, particularly when the name is shared with a Black person. In this instance, it's not just a coincidence or a point of curiosity; it's a potential reminder of America's unfinished reckoning with its past. When White people do not immediately consider the historical roots of shared last names with Black people, it points to a broader issue of historical disconnection, the tendency to avoid confronting the legacy of slavery and its lasting impact, failing to understand that shared last names between Black and White individuals often have painful origins tied to slavery, forced assimilation, and systemic inequality. It reveals a more profound truth about how history shapes identity and relationships, even when those connections are uncomfortable or unspoken. It reveals the existence of privilege.

Why does privilege matter? It matters because privilege creates a lack of equity. It is essential for those of us with privileges to understand the experiences of people who do not share our privilege. What does that feel like in the workplace? As the first or the only gay Black female in my previous workplace, I have experienced the effects of the privilege held by others many times. I saw many of the men in the workplace form fantasy sports leagues and (hopefully) unconsciously exclude the women (me included). I saw my White male peers go out to lunch together often, rarely inviting me to join the group, while I did not have a group of peers like me to have that camaraderie with. I had my suggestions ignored in meetings, only to have a male peer make the same suggestion moments later that was met with compliments about what a great idea he came up with. Those are just a few examples of how the privilege of others in the workplace—privilege that I did not share—impacted me. As my experiences demonstrate, people from underserved communities are often present in smaller numbers within the workplace. As a result, they do not have their unique needs understood or met.

ADDRESSING PRIVILEGE

My workshop about privilege is often the most uncomfortable for clients because they can get defensive at the thought of being accused of having privileges. It's important to really understand that we all have them; it's another part of our human experience. Your privilege may be growing up in a middle-class family or attending a top-tier university. Some of us are privileged to walk through this world with an abled body, while others are privileged through networks or social capital.

Guilt and shame are not productive when addressing privilege. Much like unconscious biases, having privilege does not make us bad people. What matters is how we choose to use our privileges. We can choose to reflect on our privileges and be aware of how they may impact others. We can acknowledge our privilege in conversations with other people and educate other people about their privileges. Most importantly, we can use our privileges to assist others by helping to remove barriers for people who don't share our privileges, standing up for them, and advocating for them. In other words, we can make a significant difference for people who don't share our privileges by stepping up for them and becoming their allies.

Microaggressions and privilege have been staples of workplace culture for many generations, serving as daily disruptors to the equity and inclusion that should accompany today's diverse workforce. By taking responsibility for our transgressions and speaking against these behaviors when we see them perpetrated against others, we can push against the resistance to DEI that barriers create.

CHAPTER SEVEN

The Truth About the Workplace

Here are some workplace truths that I find hard to swallow. Women are the majority population in the United States. Yet, we hold only 10.4 percent of CEO positions in Fortune 500 companies.[1,2] In 2022, 14.4 percent of the country's population self-identified as Black, yet Black CEOs head less than 2 percent of Fortune 500 companies.[3,4] People who identify as Hispanic of any race made up 19.5 percent of the population in 2023 but account for only 16 CEOs of Fortune 500 companies.[5,6] And as of 2023, only 4 Fortune 500 companies are led by openly LGBTQ+ CEOs.[7]

These statistics, while alarming, are not really surprising. And given the lack of diverse leadership at the top level of most corporations, it's not surprising that the lack of equity and inclusion remains an uncomfortable truth in the workplace.

INEQUITIES IN THE WORKPLACE

We often hear DEI critics proclaim that workplace discrimination is a thing of the past, but in reality, it is still very present. Even with the strides that have been made, there is still much work to do. According to the Equal Employment Opportunity Commission's (EEOC) Annual Report, the agency filed 143 merit lawsuits against employers in 2023, a 50 percent increase from fiscal year 2022.[8] Of those cases, 64.3 percent were brought under Title VII of the Civil Rights Act, which protects workers from discrimination based on their race, color, religion, sex, or national origin; 34.3 percent were brought under the Americans with Disabilities Act (ADA); 8.4 percent under the Age Discrimination in Employment Act; and 2.1 percent under the Equal Pay Act.

These numbers prove that workplace discrimination is still very much present, from hiring practices to pay gaps and even in day-to-day interactions. And the truth that drives this reality is that people from historically underrepresented communities are not allowed to thrive in non-inclusive workplace cultures.

Workplace inequities affect employees across all industries and roles, stemming from systemic disparities such as unequal access to opportunities and implicit biases. Women, people of color, LGBTQ+ individuals, people with disabilities, and other underrepresented groups often bear the brunt of these disparities. Sometimes, it takes place overtly, like the blatant harassment of a transgender person. Other times, it comes in the more subtle packaging of unconscious bias, such as the refusal to assign a person with physical challenges to a particular project based on assumptions about their abilities. As discussed in chapter 6, legal protections like the Civil Rights Act and the ADA have been around for years, yet the practices they seek to address remain. Enforcing legal protections can be time-consuming and challenging to prove, so many employees feel they have no choice but to tolerate discriminatory workplace practices instead of challenging them. This is particularly true in relation to subtle biases or systemic inequities, such as the gender pay gap.

Signed into law in 1963, the Equal Pay Act requires that men and women be paid equally for performing substantially equal work in the same establishment. "Equal work" refers to jobs that require "equal skill, effort, and responsibility and which are performed under similar working conditions."[9] Yet, despite this legislation, glaring pay gaps persisted, largely thanks to loopholes, such as justifications based on factors like seniority or merit systems. In 2009, the federal government passed the Lilly Ledbetter Fair Pay Act, also aimed at addressing wage inequities more comprehensively. However, legal enforcement is only one part of closing the gender wage gap. It also requires organizational transparency, which some large corporations continue to resist.

Despite years of awareness and advocacy, women, on average, still earn approximately eighty-two cents for every dollar earned by men in the United States.[10] When intersecting factors such as race and ethnicity are considered, the numbers are even more alarming, with Black women earning only seventy cents per dollar and Latina women earning only sixty-five cents per dollar.[11] These statistics exemplify the heightened disadvantage faced by women of color in the workplace.

There are numerous driving forces behind the pay gap, reflecting some of our society's inhumanities. For instance, from very young ages, girls are often funneled into lower-paying industries and roles traditionally dominated by women, such as caregiving and education. And it is no coincidence that these roles, which are so vital to our society, offer lower salaries compared to male-dominated sectors like technology, engineering, and finance. It is a division driven by generations of stereotypes and societal expectations about what professional roles are "appropriate" for women.

Unpaid labor is a significant factor in the gender pay gap discussion. Women disproportionately shoulder caregiving responsibilities like child-rearing, elder care, and household management, which limits their availability for paid employment opportunities. These "traditional" roles can also limit professional advancement due to unplanned career interruptions, the necessity to work part-time, or decisions to opt out of the workforce entirely, all of which have long-term financial repercussions.

These gender-based stereotypes can also greatly impact the experiences of women within the workforce. Implicit and explicit biases discourage assertiveness in women. When women do speak up, they may be met with resistance or viewed negatively, which can also impact performance reviews and affect promotion decisions. For women of color, the intersection of gender and racial discrimination exacerbates these challenges. Stereotypes of "angry" Black women or "fiery" Latina women can create a workplace culture where their contributions are undervalued and even dismissed.

Workplace inequities are also evident in the continuous workplace discrimination experienced by members of the LGBTQ+

community. As of 2020, more than eight million workers in the U.S. identify as LGBTQ+, but those numbers have not stopped the mistreatment and harassment that members of this community face within the workplace.[12] A 2023 report by the UCLA Williams Institute found that almost half of LGBTQ employees report experiencing instances of discrimination or harassment at work based on their sexual orientation or gender identity.[13]

Attorney Stephen Kulp serves on the National LGBTQ+ Bar Association's Board of Directors. In 2022, he received the Class of 2022 National LGBTQ+ Bar Association 40 under 40 award. Kulp says that though crossroads have been made within the workforce, the challenge lies in protecting the paths that have been paved while also making sure to pave new roads. "I find the LGBTQ+ community, on the one hand, in places of lots of power and privilege," says Stephen, "but that usually goes hand-in-hand with Whiteness and maleness. On the other hand, I see almost no or very few LGBTQ+…leaders. I mean, I'm seeing more of them for sure, but the reality is that we are a minority. And for those with intersectional identities, we are minorities within a minority and sometimes minorities within a minority within a minority."

The new roads that have yet to be paved must include workplace cultures where transgender people feel valued and welcomed. According to a 2024 study by the UCLA School of Law Williams Center, eighty-two percent of transgender Americans report experiencing some form of workplace discrimination or harassment, including termination, hiring, and promotions, as well as being subjected to verbal, physical, or sexual harassment.[14] Studies show that transgender candidates are less likely to be called back for interviews, even when their qualifications are equal to those of cisgender applicants.[15] And if employment is secured, they may encounter misgendering, invasive questions, or blatant harassment.

S. Leigh Thompson is a strategist, facilitator, and consultant on DEI issues. As they so aptly point out, the conversation around bathrooms that dominates the discussion about transgender rights is incredibly limited. "Yes, trans people have to pee," they said, "but that's not the only situation that trans folks experience. We end up just limiting it to that where people say, 'Okay, we did that for you, and now we're done.' The inclusion of trans folk has a long way to go. And that pendulum swing that we're seeing right now is a lot of virulent violence and removal of trans people from impact and influence."

For individuals, the demoralizing effects of working in an environment where you feel undervalued or excluded can be profound. It can cause incredible stress, lower job satisfaction, and even physical health issues. For organizations, a discriminatory workplace is simply bad for business. Internally, it can result in high attrition rates, employee absence, and poor work performance. Outwardly, it negatively impacts reputation and may lead to decreased revenue. And what happens within our workplaces also has societal impacts.

Leigh describes the workplace as one of our biggest learning environments that significantly impact society. "Now that we are in a more globalized culture, we have very fast communication with people in so many spaces outside of our immediate physical proximity, which then allows us to get all these ideas from all these workplaces and see what is possible. So, more than ever, the workplace has a significant impact on how we understand, learn, then repeat the structured systems of the world that we live in. If we want to treat each other with dignity, care, and respect, then we need to make sure it's embedded in not just the work that we do or the things that we say but how we engage with each other as a workplace community."

Leigh also spoke about the influence that society has on the workplace. "Even the people who are able to make it to the top who don't look like people in previous generations who've been in that top are often also still influenced by a belief system that supports a very small amount of people to get to that top," they said. "White supremacy culture impacts the idea of the way to be a professional, the way the types of ideas that we're supposed to have, the way that we're supposed to interact with each other, can still go to something that's embedded both in White folks and also folks in color. We have all been taught how to be oppressive; whether or not the oppression actually hurts us or helps us, we've all been taught how to do it, and so we can often do it to each other."

AN EVOLVING WORKPLACE

The modern workplace is more diverse than it has ever been in history, and that includes generational demographics. It is not uncommon to have an office with Baby Boomers, Generation X, Millennials, Generation Z, and, more recently, Generation Alpha, all working together. While this mixture of perspectives and experiences can be of value to an organization, it can also lead to a clash of values and expectations, resulting in conflicts and challenges around communication.

For instance, Baby Boomers tend to value loyalty and a strong work ethic. Many of them entered the workforce when career stability was expected and championed. At the other end of the spectrum, Millennials and Generation Z tend to value purpose-driven work and innovation. They grew up in a digital world and are often the most tech-savvy employees in the building. Wedged in the middle is Generation X, the sandwich generation that cares for their children and aging parents. As a result, they tend to value flexibility and work-life balance.

With all these differences, tensions can run high. Generation X employees may perceive Millennials as entitled or impatient in their promotion expectations. In contrast, Generation Z employees may view their Baby Boomer colleagues as stuck in their ways and condescending. This is an environment ripe for employment discrimination and microaggressions. Older workers in leadership positions may resist giving promotions to younger workers simply based on age. Conversely, younger workers may use technology and communication tools to create a hostile work environment for older workers.

Generational diversity can be an asset but only if organizations foster a culture of inclusion and equity. When leaders tolerate discriminatory behavior, even implicitly, it is likely to persist, even as demographics evolve.

Through my educational trainings, I have noticed another workplace evolution where a large segment of the blue-collar workforce—which is predominantly comprised of economically disadvantaged White workers and people of color—must operate with a combination of forces that make the workplace almost impossible to thrive in. Their leaders are so far removed from the everyday realities of this workforce that they have no interest in, or capacity for, caring about them in any meaningful way. They also have no incentive to address the systemic inequities that can keep these blue-collar workers from having a positive work experience.

Many in leadership positions do not feel the need to respect the people who work many, many, many rungs of the corporate ladder below them. Instead, they foster a dismissive and disrespectful environment where employees don't feel safe speaking up. These leaders do not invest in blue-collar workers' personal or professional development. Consequently, these employees carry a deep emotional wound related to their inability to move into management positions and improve their life circumstances. They remain stuck, unhappy in their jobs, and angry with their employers, which can create a hostile work environment for everyone.

Blue-collar workers have become "the forgotten" in our society and our organizations and are, therefore, on one fringe of the workplace population. That's why providing this workplace population with DEI education is important, just as it is for senior leadership and mid-level managers. Every member of the organization, no matter what position they hold, should be provided with an understanding of how to interact with their co-workers who may be different or sometimes completely foreign to them, and they need to see that the organization holds everyone accountable for maintaining an inclusive culture, including leadership.

The workforce population on the other fringe are leaders who place themselves on a pedestal, insulated by their wealth. Their financial status limits their exposure to people at different income levels, which generally means they spend most, if not all, their time with people just like themselves. As a result, they don't have meaningful interactions with the people they lead or even individuals in financial situations similar to those they lead.

I have noticed that each fringe population has a minimal understanding of what engaging with other populations is like because they're so insulated within their own experiences and communities. They are cut off from one another with no understanding of the challenges they each face. That lack of personal understanding leads them to rely entirely on biases seeded by stereotypes in how they think and feel about the other group. People at the top of the organizational chart may fear people who aren't like them and of losing their power. People on the opposite end may be afraid and angry because they've never had power and feel like they will never have it in their current circumstances. They likely feel disenfranchised.

The truth is that to create a truly inclusive environment where everyone feels welcome, respected, and valued and believes they can thrive, we need to think about how we can bring people across the workplace—including those on both ends of the workplace fringes—into the DEI conversation. How do we bridge the gap between them and help them not be so afraid or angry with each other based on assumptions and stereotypes?

WHY ORGANIZATIONS NEED TO TAKE ACTION

In the course of one day in October 2024, the EEOC's Philadelphia District Office filed lawsuits against three different businesses for race-based discrimination practices and retaliation against employees who complained about discrimination.[16] Organizations that don't prioritize an equitable and inclusive culture increase the risk of discrimination occurring within the workplace, which also increases the risk of resulting legal action. The fact that workplace discrimination cases rose in 2024 indicates a greater need now than ever for employers to focus on building equitable and inclusive workplaces for both moral and business reasons.[17] This is why looking closely at employment practices is so important. An organization may not be on the losing end of a workplace discrimination lawsuit yet, but with an inequitable corporate culture and immoral business practices, it may just be a matter of time.

CHAPTER EIGHT

The Truth About Legal Protections

As a Black gay woman born before the passsage of the Civil Rights Act of 1964, I am very familiar with the reality of living in a society where the laws of the land do not protect my basic rights. Though I was a young child during the 1960s, I do have some memories of "White only" signs and having to pee on the lawn in the South because my mother wouldn't let me go into the colored bathrooms that were never cleaned. To this day, I vividly recall the warnings of my grandmother about the KKK marching down the street, and I still feel the sting of the constant isolation that came with balancing the judgments of my race and complexion.

As I got older and embraced my sexual identity, I discovered that my intersectionality meant that, just by being who I was born to be, I needed protection from the government in order to be considered a whole person. And though policies have been enacted throughout my life to protect my rights in different ways, I know that they are there at the whim of political powers, which means that my rights as a Black gay woman are constantly in danger.

A WHOLE PERSON

By the time I turned twenty-one, I was out of my parents' house and on my own. I was paying bills and was responsible for myself and my well-being, so I felt freer to explore my sexuality and take risks. I figured I would just be who I was because trying to be anything else was exhausting. But even with my willingness to embrace my true self, I dipped in and out of shame and fear, especially when it came to work. It was the eighties, a time when being a gay woman could cost you a job, so I had to practice some careful discretion. It is horrible trying to live two different lives, deprived of the ability to bring all of yourself to work or your friendships. How do you feel good about yourself when you're lying about who you are?

I remember an incident when I first started practicing law. I was an associate at the time, and one of the partners was getting married. I had my father fly out from California to accompany me to the wedding because I wasn't comfortable taking a woman with me as my date. I felt an overwhelming insecurity because there was no one else like me in any regard. Yes, there were other women, but there were no other Black people or gay people. I felt compelled to compromise who I was, and it was a horrible thing to do. Most people in the LGBTQ+ community have their journey around coming to terms with their truth. What feels safe, and what doesn't feel safe. What they're willing to compromise and what they are not willing to compromise.

It took me quite a while to get through that journey entirely in terms of caring what it might cost. I was completely out when I began my career with professional sports teams. But there were no legal protections for me. If they wanted to fire me for being gay, they could have because it would have been perfectly legal for them to do so. I decided that, from a cost-benefit analysis, it was more important for me to be healthy and show up as my authentic self than it was to worry about getting fired. I resolved to trust the journey and the process. If they wanted to fire me for being gay, it was not an organization that I wanted to work for anyway.

Before the first protections came in place, I was the lawyer at the Diamondbacks. When I looked at the employee manual and realized that there were no protections for people based on sexual orientation, I decided to ask my boss if we could add them. He agreed, and I felt protected. It wasn't just about me, though. Although I was the only one truly out, I knew other people were not out or as vocal about it. We made the additions, and the changes were obviously appreciated. I saw people within the organization become more comfortable and vocal about their lives, their partners, or their spouses. I was really grateful that I worked for an organization that was willing to provide that type of protection, even though they weren't legally required to do so.

When the employment discrimination laws eventually changed, it was amazing. It felt like we were finally on the road to being treated as whole people instead of "less than" everyone else. And when the Supreme Court legalized same-sex marriage in June 2015, I was absolutely over the moon. It always baffled my mind that I was not entitled to marry someone I loved because others did not agree with it. And who were they to legislate my life? At the time, I had no interest in being married. I wasn't seeing anyone seriously at the time, and I didn't even know I would ever want to marry someone, but I was still infuriated by being told I could not do so. That Supreme Court decision and the legislative changes that followed meant that I finally had the right to have the same legal protections for my relationships that heterosexual people do… I was thrilled and finally felt like a whole person.

PROTECTIONS FOR TWENTY PERCENT OF THE POPULATION

Dawna Callahan has been blazing trails for people with disabilities since childhood. A wheelchair user since the age of three, when Dawna experienced incomplete paralysis as a result of transverse myelitis, a neurological disorder that causes inflammation of the spinal cord. She was the first student with a physical disability mainstreamed into her Bay Area school district in California. "I always say I taught my teachers as much as they taught me because we had to figure this out as we went along," said Dawna, who remembers the fight for equal public access prior to the passage of the Americans with Disabilities Act (ADA) in 1990. "We had to go to the town council to get ramps put in so that I could walk to school with my brother and not have to take the short bus." She explained that though the cost of five ramps was only about $250.00 at the time, council members still questioned whether they could justify the cost for one student.

On July 26, 1990, President George H.W. Bush signed the ADA into law, prohibiting discrimination based on disability, just as other civil rights laws prohibit discrimination based on race, color, sex, national origin, age, and religion. The legislation includes five sections, each governing accommodation requirements for different types of organizations:

- The Employment title governs employers with fifteen or more employees. It states they "must provide people with disabilities an equal opportunity to benefit from the employment-related opportunities available to others."
- The State and Local Government title requires that even the smallest local governments provide people with disabilities equal access to all offered programs, services, and activities.
- The Public Transit Systems title requires equal opportunity for accessibility of all public transportation for people with disabilities.
- The Businesses that are Open to the Public title requires businesses like restaurants, hotels, stores, gyms, and private schools to provide people with disabilities an equal opportunity to access the goods or services they offer.
- The Telecommunication Companies title requires telecommunications companies to provide services that allow callers with hearing and speech disabilities to communicate.

Dawna started her graduate degree program in industrial organizational psychology just as the ADA was passed into law. "It was an interesting time for people with disabilities," she said, "Lots of discussion, papers, and research about reasonable accommodation. And sadly, we still have those conversations thirty-plus years later. I had the fortunate experience of working with a woman named Deb Dagit. She's a little person who was at the signing of the ADA, and she hired me as an intern in Silicon Valley to work on what we called, at the time, strategic cultural initiatives. I didn't have a lot of people to look toward when I started my professional career. I spent a lot of time and energy trying to fit in and not bring attention to my disability. I had to create a world where I could function and be successful."

After completing her first graduate degree, Dawna took out a personal loan to buy herself a mono-ski, which allows for skiing in a sitting position. Each weekend, she loaded up her four-wheel drive Ford Explorer and headed to the slopes of Lake Tahoe. Not only did she find connections with people who shared her passions and love for life, but she also found a purpose that would pivot her professional journey. Dawna returned to graduate school to earn a master's in recreation management and began her work in a field where much work was left to do, even with the protections of the ADA in place.

In 2017, Dawna founded All In Sport Consulting, a consulting firm that leads organizations in creating life-changing opportunities for people with disabilities through adapted sport. "Before starting my firm, I had previously worked for a national disability sport organization where I was the only person on the leadership team with a disability," Dawna said. "And even though I represented the community, I always felt like I was swimming upstream." Dawna shared that disability representation is lacking in the spaces of adapted sport or paralympic sport. "You would never see that at an NAACP chapter. You would never see some White dude leading a Hispanic Chamber of Commerce. So why is this okay? Did the disability community hand that over? Do we not have a professional pipeline? Do we not have retired Paralympian athletes?"

To address this lack of workplace diversity, Dawna often intersects her sport business with her human resources background to advocate for people with disabilities in the workplace. "I've worked for all four national sport organizations that are multi-sport, multi disability, including US Paralympics, which falls within the US Olympic and Paralympic Committee. And to be honest with you, I always reported to someone without a disability except for one organization," Dawna said.

The ADA had a profound effect on the protection of rights for people with disabilities, yet there is still much work to do. Discrimination still exists within public facilities, the workplace, and society in general. People with disabilities also deal with the underlying biases and microaggressions of a toxic work environment.

Dawna recalled an infuriating incident that occurred at an organizational leadership dinner. "The board president at the time, one of the leaders within the organization, patted me on the head. I've been an advocate for people with disabilities all my life, both athletes and professionals, but I was so shocked that I just froze. I couldn't say anything. I think it's like when a woman is sexually harassed, you're just taken aback. You're in shock and don't know what to do. If no one else was patted on the head that night, that's what we refer to as ableism in our world, which is the discrimination against people with disabilities, intentional or unintentional.

Maybe he was just pleased with the work I was doing and felt that he was acknowledging that, but there are other ways to do it. I'm a professional woman, and I've put in a lot of years." Dawna said that after a little bit of a meltdown, she realized that the organization did not align with who she was and decided to leave. She now helps others fight against this type of treatment, both inside and outside of adapted sports.

"The disability community is still not included in DEI conversations, and yet it's fifteen to twenty percent of the population," Dawna explained. "That's almost one in every household, including visible and invisible disabilities. And it's not included because we don't understand it's intersectional. You could be a Latina and a lesbian with cerebral palsy. It intersects with all the other communities. The disabled population is one that anybody can become a part of at any time in life through an injury, accident, or diagnosis. Not to be a Debbie Downer, but it's something that happens on a daily basis throughout the world. A thirty-five-year-old mom receiving an MS diagnosis or an eighteen-year-old high school soccer star with a cancer diagnosis having to navigate life with an amputated leg. People with disabilities are tired of tiptoeing around this conversation. I have people ask me, 'What do we call you?' Call me a person. Call me a woman. Call me a professional."

The legal protections of the ADA did a lot to provide people with disabilities better access within a world that largely disregards their basic needs. However, legislation alone did not prevent nor end Dawna's feelings of being stifled and oppressed within the workplace. Her experiences exemplify why so much work remains left to be done. "In all my previous positions, I've had to fit into leadership's box. And when leaders don't have a disability, they don't have that lived experience. They turn the lights off at night, lock the door, and leave the office. They don't have people at Target asking them if they need help. They don't have people calling them an inspiration for simply getting in and out of their car or any of the other garbage that people with disabilities do on a daily basis to advocate for the community."

LEGAL PROTECTIONS UNDER ATTACK

Legal protection simply isn't enough on its own. The overturning of *Roe v. Wade* showed us that protections are not guaranteed because laws can be changed. The Voting Rights Act has been weakened substantially by loopholes like gerrymandering and restrictive state voting laws, and continuous attacks on privacy protections put LGBTQ+ rights at constant risk. Legal protection becomes nothing more than words on paper when those in power manipulate the rules to remove their enforcement and spread false rhetoric to villainize the purpose behind the laws. Unless people really understand why these protections remain necessary and are willing to live by them, they don't matter.

Under the first Donald Trump administration, we witnessed a wave of societal and political thinking that completely set back efforts toward equity and inclusion in our country. He empowered White supremacists in a way that they hadn't been before in modern history. They were always there, lurking in the shadows but not doing much harm because they didn't have the seat of government in their back pocket. Trump empowered fear and hate in ways that we hadn't seen since before the Civil Rights Act of 1964 was passed. His administration put people and mechanisms in place to turn things back and regain control over people from whom control had been lost. That is even truer now in his second administration.

Seeing our rights as women to make decisions about our bodies taken away awakened many women to some truths about our society. The right to an abortion is not of personal importance to me because I'm well past that age. But whether you want to do it or not, you should have the right to make the best choice for you and your family. I never thought we'd lose *Roe v. Wade*, and in some ways, it feels like imprisonment. Women are no longer free to do with their bodies what they would choose. Trump has loaded the courts with judges who are willing to adjudicate based on religion, and voters have loaded the legislative houses with politicians who are willing to legislate humanity with disregard for people's lives.

The truth of the matter is that the same people harshly judging transgender people and trying to legislate who people in the LGBTQ+ community can love are the same people who hold up the religious flag as the basis for their discriminatory actions. They choose to legislate judgment instead of legislating equity. I went through twelve years of Catholic school, and I am sure the Bible said, "Judge, not lest ye be judged." Yet they are doing unspeakable things, all in the name of religion. To this day, I am still trying to figure all of this out, but I simply cannot accept the hypocrisy… the same hypocrisy that currently puts so many of our civil rights at risk.

Until there is equity, until there is full inclusion, we are not free. That's the bottom line with race relations, LGBTQ+ issues, women's rights—all of it. I am tremendously concerned that the rights that we have seen protected under the law will be taken away based on a desire to maintain power and control. It's so hurtful. Who are you to tell me that I'm less than a whole person because of the color of my skin or the texture of my hair? And who are you to tell me that I can't have the same rights as you because I love someone of my same gender? Who are you to tell someone they cannot pursue their chosen career because they are a person with a disability?

We're taking giant steps backward—maybe even running backward! That is why I am grateful to be able to do my work, and it makes me really want to double down in my efforts to shine a light on the TRUTH. I obviously can't make people hire me, but I will keep doing the work because it's more important now than ever.

THE RIGHT TO BE A PERSON

The moral case for legal protections is that it's simply the right thing to do. Everybody should have access to the same things and opportunities to be treated like everyone else. It would be lovely if we didn't have to have laws to enforce that. After all, why would we need the Voting Rights Act of 1965 if everyone could vote? Systemic oppression was written into the United States Constitution and other laws to maintain control and power over people deemed to be inferior by people who deemed themselves to be superior in all respects.

Living in a society where you feel like you never have the right to be whole is infuriating. Is that not the very definition of enslavement? We are governed by a group of predominantly White cis-gendered, non-disabled men, most of whom aren't even aware of what oppression feels like. They don't even think about it because they don't have to, and that's where so many people get lost. Those born with certain privileges are insulated from experiencing a world without these protections, so they never have to think about them. They think, "Well, you have your legal rights," with no consideration for the consequences of those rights not being evenly applied or even enforced at all.

I don't believe that the majority of people just don't care. I think that they are instead asleep … blissfully unaware of what people who are not like them carry and confront every single day. This is why education and understanding is so important. We must open people's eyes to the truth that others experience and double down on not only the existence of legal protections but also their required enforcement. It is the only way we will get meaningful and sustainable change.

Taking Action

CHAPTER NINE

The Truth About the Business Imperative

At the start of 2025, Forbes published an alarming list of corporations that have announced plans to abandon all or part of their diversity programs.[1] Included in the list were Amazon's plans to roll back employee programs addressing "specific disparities;" Meta, which made a very public announcement about ending equity and inclusion employee trainings, as well as diversity hiring efforts; Walmart's abandonment of its DEI commitments, including the removal of certain LGBTQ+-themed products from its website and ending participation in the Human Rights Campaign's external surveys; and Molson Coors, a company that defended a feminist-themed ad campaign against conservative ridicule in 2023 and received a perfect score from the Human Rights Campaign for its LGBTQ+ policies. Yet, in 2025, Molson Coors announced its decision to halt supplier diversity programs, along with its participation in diversity surveys.

While these decisions to push back against workplace diversity feel alarming, they do nothing to change the trajectory of the American workforce and the challenges that all companies, including the ones listed in the Forbes article, will face as our population continues to become more diverse. According to the US Census Bureau, by 2043, the United States will become a majority-minority nation for the first time, and that comes with many implications for businesses.[2] By halting DEI efforts and backsliding on promises, these companies are establishing a record for themselves that will not be forgotten or overlooked by the younger generations of consumers and employees. The shortsightedness of making decisions based on today's political landscape will negatively impact these companies in the years to come.

DECONSTRUCTING THE BACKLASH

Many DEI reversals have come from corporate America's response to political backlash. When McDonald's, which was also included in the Forbes article, announced the renaming of its diversity team to "Global Inclusion Team," the company cited the Supreme Court decision *Students for Fair Admissions v. Harvard*, which held that race-based affirmative action programs in college admissions violate the equal protection clause of the Fourteenth Amendment, effectively ending affirmative action at universities.[3] While the decision specifically targeted both public and private colleges, the case has far-reaching effects on DEI programs in workplaces, further complicated by presidential executive orders and Department of Justice

(DOJ) directives that target what they egregiously characterize as "illegal discrimination" within DEI programs. Educational institutions, both private and public, corporations, government contractors, and even federal agencies have been forced to carefully navigate threats to their federal funding if they do not comply.

Attorney David M. Dixon is a Truth DEI senior consultant who has been tracking the trajectory of diversity and inclusion court cases for years. He says that the seminal legal case for affirmative action was *UC Berkley v. Baake*, which was decided in 1978. While the Supreme Court held that racial quotas were unconstitutional, it did allow the use of race as one of several factors in college admission considerations. David says that the 2023 Students for Fair Admissions case upended forty years of legal precedent with one decision. "In my read of it, though [the Supreme Court] didn't exactly overturn it, they put a stranglehold on it," he said. "It's still viable, but it might as well have been overturned because it opened up permission for organizations to backpedal or really just stand as who they truly were in the first place."

"In 2020, we saw this surge for investment in support of diversity, inclusion, belonging, and social justice," says David. "I used to describe it as a tsunami wave, which was awesome. I hadn't seen that in my lifetime, so I wanted to ride the wave and gain as much ground as possible. There was an uptick in companies bringing on DEI people and an uptick of diverse people being promoted to the C-suite level, but now we are starting to see that go backward. We didn't expect it to stay at that level of energy with George Floyd and Breonna Taylor and Black Lives Matter forever, but at the same time, the legal system has made it even harder. I have quite a few friends who work in DEI in different industries, and when the Supreme Court decision came out, they were told to sit still. To stop doing their work and hand over documents to the general counsel's office and the legal team for them to review."

Along with the legal attacks on DEI, these companies are also responding to a conservative backlash against anything labeled as "woke." We've seen this in boycotts organized against companies like Bud Light for collaborating with a transgender influencer and Disney for speaking out against Florida's "Don't Say Gay" bill. These protests often start with social media campaigns, where "otherness" is championed by algorithms and siloed thinking. They exemplify the truth about our inhumanity that we spoke about in Chapter Two. However, as Plato once pointed out, an empty vessel can make the loudest sound. We have reached a point in our society where our most prominent corporations are making decisions based on the actions of a few individuals with large social media platforms.

DEI IS NOT GOING AWAY

Among the bad news about large corporations who have abandoned DEI policies, there is good reason for hope, given the corporations that have refused to back down. In January 2025, Costco's board of directors unanimously came out in favor of upholding the company's DEI commitments, and Apple's board took a similar stance.[4] In addition, many American corporations continue to have DEI policies in place, many with plans to increase their efforts.

These companies understand the long game that companies like Walmart and Meta are missing.

The population of this country is constantly evolving. Over the next few decades, these companies will find themselves at a tremendous disadvantage, having to play catch-up with organizations that have established themselves as diverse and inclusive places to work and patronize. From an employment standpoint, they are rolling back programs even though they have not yet created a culture that enables people who are not in the current majority to succeed. If they can't see themselves succeeding there, if they don't feel welcome, they're not going to come work for these companies now or in the future.

Gen Z candidates pay close attention to which companies walk the walk regarding diversity and inclusion, with more than 80 percent considering an organization's DEI track record when choosing an employer.[5] Along with Millennials and Generation Alpha, Generation Z is the future of the workforce, and as the most racially and ethnically diverse generations in American history, they have much higher expectations around diversity. These generations recognize the importance of DEI and are not willing to compromise when choosing an employer. These generations have also grown up in a world where sexual orientation is far less shunned, so they want to work for organizations that respect their differences and treat all employees fairly, regardless of their diversity. Attracting and retaining this generation of workers will be imperative in the coming years, providing a solid business case for maintaining DEI practices and policies.

Companies that choose to roll back diversity efforts will ultimately regret going backward at a time when they need to keep moving forward due to demographic evolution, changes in values, and changes in consumer buying power. They will either do the work now or have to play catch-up later before they lose relevance in a changing world.

From a consumer perspective, people want to support brands that share their values. The homogenous marketplace of yesterday has evolved into an assortment of diverse cultures, perspectives, and interests. Not only are historically underrepresented communities accounting for a larger percentage of the population, but their economic power is also increasing substantially. Since 2000, all diverse consumer markets have grown faster than the buying power of White people. Black buying power rose to $1.6 trillion in 2020, representing the second biggest diverse market after Hispanic people.[6] The buying power of LGBTQ+ Americans has surpassed $1.3 trillion.[7]

Women control $6.4 trillion in US consumer spending that keeps companies afloat.[8] They drive seventy to eighty percent of all consumer purchasing decisions. Additionally, 1 million culturally diverse immigrants enter the United States annually and spend over $2 trillion annually.[9,10] These groups have reshaped the landscape of modern markets with their purchasing power, and their buying decisions will impact the success of corporate America in the decades ahead.

When companies fail to be inclusive of these consumers through diverse leadership, community investment, DEI initiatives, and representative branding and marketing, they risk significant financial loss because investment in underserved communities not only builds brand loyalty but also drives sustainable growth in emerging markets. If organizations are not inclusive of these consumers in terms of representation (diverse leadership), investment in their communities, DEI initiatives, branding, and marketing, they are leaving a considerable amount of money on the table.

STAYING THE COURSE

As organizations make decisions about the future of their DEI efforts, one trend we see is the rebranding of DEI policies under a different name. Terms like *belonging*, *global*, and *fairness* are being used instead, though the underlying policies sometimes remain the same. We also see the term *inclusion* being used on its own in place of DEI as another way to rebrand the work in a way that detractors will find more palatable.

Many individuals and business leaders are terrified of the term *DEI*, but we cannot let our fear overtake our commitment to doing the work. In all candor, as a business owner, I contemplated whether I should rename Truth DEI Consulting in the interest of not losing potential business. I ultimately decided to keep it because DEI is the very core of what we do; it is our truth, and we will not be inauthentic about our truth in order to make others more comfortable. I did that for much too long as a gay person in corporate America. I will not do it now.

I understand not everyone will agree with my position, and I respect their absolute right to disagree. What is most important is that we do the work, whatever you want to call it! The truth is that most companies really first need to focus on creating an equitable and inclusive culture that will support diversity before they focus on becoming more diverse. Otherwise, they will continue to spin their wheels with the performative efforts we have so often seen and will continue to be unable to attract and retain top talent from diverse backgrounds. That will be highly problematic for them in this changing world.

I end this chapter with a quote from David that sums up this conversation beautifully. When asked if DEI is going away, he responded, "It is never going away, but what we will see in the next few years is which companies were really invested in inclusion and which ones were not."

CHAPTER TEN

The Truth About Taking Action

Throughout this book, we have taken a deep look at why DEI is so important and why it will remain so in the years to come. We have explored ourselves, our workplaces, and our society regarding issues of equity and inclusion for all people. We've debunked the myth about DEI going away and identified why it remains a business imperative that should compel all organizations to not only continue their DEI efforts but even double down on them as we move into a changing world.

Now, we'll explore some of the actions organizations and organizational leaders can take to move toward a more inclusive culture that will thrive in the years to come.

FROM THE TOP DOWN

A successful DEI strategy must start from the top leadership levels; otherwise, it will never work. Some people think that just means the CEO, which is obviously an important piece of the puzzle, but it also includes every leadership team member. If your workforce does not see DEI efforts modeled by every leader, individuals will not comprehend its importance. This lack of cohesion can leave some employees feeling empowered to discount new DEI programs while others feel let down by the lack of enforcement. CEOs must be willing to hold their leadership team accountable for both modeling and enforcing expected behaviors around equity and inclusion for everyone.

A C-suite leadership retreat is among my top recommendations when working with clients. These experiences allow leaders to tuck themselves away for two or three days with a DEI leader who can help facilitate the conversation around diversity, equity, inclusion, and belonging within the organization. I call it a systemic cleanse that evolves the leadership team towards a more inclusive and equitable future.

Change can be uncomfortable, and sometimes hard decisions will have to be made regarding accountability for one's actions, as well as the actions of every other member of the organization. Every leader must recognize that the only way they get through to the other side of equity and inclusion and create a culture of belonging is to do it. That doesn't mean it can't be done with kindness, education, and gentle reminders to people, but leaders must be willing to stay the course and lead by example. Every leader should leave such a retreat with a better understanding of the importance of DEI, a clear strategy aligned with and embedded in the organizational strategic plan, and a clear and unified message to the entire organization about organization-wide expectations.

In this changing world, leadership team education is key, and it's best that it happens on the front end of the DEI strategizing. Not to be exclusive of everyone else, but educating and aligning the leadership team in a setting where they are comfortable being open and vulnerable is important. Even in that setting, all leaders may not initially be comfortable with the discussion. Part of that journey for them is also understanding that it may be uncomfortable, but it's okay to be uncomfortable through learning. That discomfort won't last forever.

Another part of the DEI leadership journey is the agreement to commit the time, people, resources, and real money necessary to really implement a DEI strategy in your organization. That takes several forms, such as a review of practices and procedures, a really deep dive to see where the blind spots are, and an understanding of where unconscious bias has crept in (oftentimes in hiring practices). That also includes a review of the employee handbook for any language that unintentionally excludes people and a review for pay equity to determine if it really exists and, if it doesn't, develop a strategy to address the inequities.

Organizations should also strongly consider the development of Employee Resource Groups (ERGs). ERGs are important because they give people a place to discuss common issues, have conversations and community, and feel seen and heard. ERGs should not be exclusive to anyone. Though they focus on a common group or issue, they should be open to all, including those interested in the group because of a personal connection and/or the group's allies.

For example, at the Diamondbacks, our LGBTQ+ ERG had a good mix of members of that community, along with straight people, cisgender people, and those who cared deeply about the issue for their own reasons. ERGs can also ultimately become Business Resource Groups (BRGs) that help connect the organization to the respective communities and help the organization better understand the communities' needs. All these things contribute to a checks and balance system that furthers DEI efforts.

THE DO'S AND DON'TS OF TAKING ACTION

- Do have a C-suite DEI leadership retreat, such as a TRUTH Retreat (see the end of this chapter for more information), to learn about DEI together and discuss vision, mission, and alignment with organizational strategy.
- Do consider similar retreats for all management-level employees. It is an investment in your culture and invaluable for aligning all leaders.
- Do invest in an outside DEI consultant to review the organization from top to bottom and make recommendations to help the organization become more inclusive.
- Do add a DEI professional to the C-suite as part of the leadership team.
- Do hold everyone in the organization accountable for equitable and inclusive behavior.
- Do provide DEI education to all staff.
- Do form and support employee resource groups (ERGs).

- Don't ignore that the world is changing in ways that DEI is now a business imperative.
- Don't engage in DEI if you're not all in with a one hundred percent commitment from the entire leadership team.
- Don't underestimate the necessary commitment of time and resources (human and monetary).
- Don't just focus on diversity; focus on building an equitable and inclusive culture supporting diversity.
- Don't be afraid to make mistakes.
- Don't let the discomfort of change keep you from working through the growing pains.

THE TRUTH ABOUT THE ROLE OF DEI PROFESSIONAL

DEI professionals do this important work because they live in their purpose and understand how important it is for businesses and their employees. They pour their heart and soul into what they do out of a genuine desire to help create a diverse, equitable, and inclusive culture where everyone belongs and can thrive, and the organization can flourish as a result. The unfortunate truth is that whether they are internal employees or external consultants, DEI professionals are often set up for failure.

If retained externally, the organization may not want to pay them what they are worth and, if they do, may refuse to implement recommendations and terminate the relationship with the consultant, blaming the lack of progress on the consultant. If hired internally, DEI professionals are often not empowered with what they need to do their jobs. They are often saddled with other responsibilities, so they can't focus on the work or are not provided with the authority or resources to do the very thing they've been hired to do. It is important to think about these things when you commit to hiring a DEI expert.

Attorney Bendita Cynthia Malakia is a lawyer, coach, and president of the National LGBTQ+ Bar. She is also an incredible global justice, equity, diversity, and inclusion strategist who graciously offered her guidance as my first mentor within the DEI space. Having worked with and within numerous organizations, Bendita has a unique grasp on the challenges that DEI professionals face in the workforce as they wrestle to succeed in what she calls "an asinine job."

"Especially when you're inside of an organization, you need to be too many people, and you need to be doing too many things, and you need to have too many skills at a level of excellence that isn't really required of any other job," Bendita says. "People want you to be able to train. So, you need to understand training methodology, best practices, and how to connect with people. Then, you have to have the subject matter expertise where people want you to deliver on all sorts of subjects, which may not be proximate to your own experience."

Bendita continues, "Your senior leadership wants you to be a trusted advisor. They want to see that you understand how the whole business operates and how what you're doing supports it. And not just supports it in the broad business case for diversity. They want to make sure that you understand how the sales transformation program and other changes they are making will elevate the business and how DEI is integrated into that. And if they do not view you as an equal, they're not going to listen to you. But that's also a big lift because you are mostly working with people who are not from historically underrepresented groups."

She goes on to say, "Then you've got the junior folks within the business who may be more diverse, and they want you to speak their language, too. It doesn't matter whether it's an Asian American Pacific Islander person; an indigenous person, an individual from Seoul, Korea; or an immigrant in London. They all want to feel like you understand their issues implicitly and will advocate for them. Then you need to win the talent war, and it all needs to look flawless. The job is ridiculous."

Bendita's explanation may give some insight into why DEI professionals have substantial turnover rates. Practitioners get burned out, especially when they're put in a position where their hiring was a performative show for the organization. It does no good to bring in a person at a mid-level or junior position to do work that they have no power or resources to do. They have no budget or authority, and people don't take them seriously because they don't have enough seniority. It's just a performative waste of time.

This is why a chief diversity officer should be a core member of the executive team, a C-suite leader with the authority and credibility to do the work while not being expected to divide their attention by managing other full-time functions. To support their success, organizations must ensure that their internal DEI leaders have the authority and resources they need, free of roadblocks so that all members recognize their position as a core function of the business. Just as the chief development officer, chief revenue officer, and chief financial officer have core and critical roles in the organization, so does the chief diversity officer. Honor that by hiring someone at the top level and empowering them to do their job. And yes, I understand that leaders can do more than one job, such as a chief financial officer who also takes on the role of chief administrative officer. However, how much better could someone in the C-suite perform if they could focus on their area of expertise? And what a powerful message you would send if DEI were valued enough to have one person in the C-suite giving it their undivided attention.

Many organizations make the mistake of placing their DEI department under human resources, a decision that greatly concerns me because, under this model, DEI never gets the attention it needs. The main focus of HR is hiring, promotions, and terminations, and though DEI can be involved in each of those areas, it is much bigger than that or should be if an organization is doing DEI correctly. DEI should be part of the overall organizational strategy and woven throughout the organization's fabric. Think about a professional sports team that has to make decisions about matters pertaining to employees, the community, the fan base, and suppliers; DEI plays a part in each of those things. In this changing world, DEI is not a nice to have; it's a must-have.

If you are serious about making DEI a core part of your organizational strategy, make critical and sometimes hard decisions. It's about investing in the success of your organization.

BREAKING DOWN BARRIERS

One of the biggest obstacles to people engaging in DEI is the fear of making a mistake. We all make mistakes, including DEI professionals. Why? Because we're human. We are all still learning and unlearning what we've been taught over our lifetimes, so errors will be made. That's just part of the learning journey. What's important is that we do better once we know better.

One way to break down the barrier of fear is to take small steps toward creating a more inclusive environment. I remember walking into a law firm for a conference I was attending. It was a beautiful lobby area filled with that old-style law firm décor. While I waited to be called back, I turned to sit in the waiting area and was welcomed by life-sized portraits of three much older White men. That was the only artwork there. I completely understand, as the portraits must have been of the firm's founders since they held such a place of singular prominence and reverence. However, as a woman of color walking into that firm, I wondered whether this was a firm that would welcome my business. If I had been there to apply for a job, I certainly would not have felt an immediate sense of belonging and would have wondered if there were other people like me there, if I would be welcome there, and if I could succeed there. You may think it is just artwork, but it is so much more than that.

How often have you waited in a doctor's office where all the artwork and magazines are about golfing, skiing, or fishing off a yacht? Those sound pretty harmless, right? Considering that those sports are costly activities that probably exclude much of their clientele, why not create a waiting room that is more inclusive of the people they serve? Yes, even artwork and magazines matter in creating an inclusive environment, so why not start there? What about the physical configuration of your office? Is it inclusive for people in the disability community, or is it filled with barriers to movement, safety, and accommodation?

TRUTH RETREATS: AN IMMERSIVE EXPERIENCE

At Truth DEI Consulting, we regularly facilitate educational workshops for our clients that typically last from one hour to half a day. And we are happy to educate our clients in the way that best fits their needs. But we also wanted to do something different that no one else was doing. From conversations I had with people who have had the opportunity to immerse themselves in the culture of another country for two to three months to learn a language, I started thinking about the power of immersive learning. HudsonWay Immersion School is an educational center that offers a complete immersion in Mandarin and Spanish education for children aged two through eighth grade in New York and New Jersey. While reading about the program and its effects on students, I found interesting correlations between the immersion experience and increased cultural sensitivity. Immersion students tend to show more positive attitudes toward other cultures and exhibit a heightened appreciation of others.

After learning about immersion education, I thought, "If that can work for education in general, why not for DEI education and strategy development?"

In 2023, the late Arthur Leon Burnette of Civil Rights Trail Tours and I joined forces, leveraging my DEI expertise and his tour and civil rights expertise, to launch Truth Retreats, an immersive, courageous leadership retreat. Truth Retreats is currently hosted in Montgomery and Selma, Alabama, and includes an immersive journey into the crucial historical context of the African American experience. The Truth Retreats team takes attendees on a three- to four-day immersive expedition towards self-discovery, understanding, and reconciliation seen through the lens of history and culture. By confronting our past and mapping out a path to healing, we believe we can collectively shape a better world rooted in fairness, equity, inclusion, and justice. And we believe these principles apply in the workplace as well.

Although focused primarily on the African American experience, we encourage attendees to use the same curiosity, empathy, cultural humility, and strategies they develop at Truth Retreats with other historically marginalized groups. Our retreats include workshops, strategy sessions, and tours, and we help attendees unlock their personal and professional power to discover, individually and collectively (in the case of a single organization), the key issues they need to address and begin to build strategies for addressing them.

Key components of Truth Retreats are visits to the Legacy Museum, National Memorial for Peace and Justice, Freedom Memorial Sculpture Park, and Southern Poverty Law Center in Montgomery, Alabama, where we exercise our empathy muscles and develop a deep, eye-opening, life-changing understanding of the African American experience, both historical and present day. The retreat also includes visiting Selma, Alabama, a city with a profound civil rights legacy, where attendees can empower themselves to do the work ahead by walking in the footsteps of Giants across the Edmund Pettis Bridge. At the conclusion of the tour experience, we provide an intensive half-day workshop to help participants determine the next steps in their journey and begin to map out their personal and organizational strategies for creating communities and cultures that are welcoming and inclusive of everyone. We continue the journey with our attendees with six monthly cohort meetings to continue the educational journey and serve as a resource for the work our attendees are doing.

Truth DEI senior consultant David Dixon, one of the retreat leaders, perfectly stated, "There's a difference between reading about the great pyramids, looking at pictures of them, seeing them in a movie, and standing at the foot of them." If you are ready to stand at the foot of history, visit our website at www.truth-retreats.com.

Humanity

CHAPTER ELEVEN

The Truth is…We are all Capable of Doing Better if We So Choose

The truth is that doing better doesn't have to be hard. People make it hard because they fear change, especially when it involves diversity, equity, and inclusion. It all comes down to whether we have the capacity and decency to care about and exercise empathy for people different from us. Our humanity is the human condition we all share, including our ability to demonstrate understanding and compassion for one another. It is the channel through which we form connections and build a society grounded in mutual care and respect.

When we recognize the humanity in one another—when we can see each other as living, feeling human beings—it inspires us to work to stand against the world's injustices. We care about when others are treated unfairly when they are hurting, and when they cannot meet their basic human needs because of the inequities they have faced. The kindness we express through small, meaningful gestures creates a ripple effect of goodwill. Even through small actions, we can rise above our individual interests to nurture one another and leave a legacy of purpose for future generations.

WE ARE ALL DEALING WITH SOMETHING

Life is complex, and we each deal with our struggles, fears, and pains. Whether it's personal loss, financial stress, health issues, or emotional burdens, we fight our battles, often silently. And those battles can be further complicated when systemic inequities amplify the challenges people from historically underrepresented and marginalized communities must face. The structural barriers that exist for some mean that their struggles are not only personal but also rooted in societal systems that further complicate the healing process.

Attorney Stephen Kulp spoke about the challenges he faces in his intersectional identity. "As an LGBTQ+ person, we have our chosen family," Stephen said. "We have those who we sought out or seek out to be the type of brother or sister or sometimes the nuclear family that non-LGBTQ+ folks have. It's based in the history of the LGBTQ+ community not being accepted by their family."

Stephen explained that he immigrated from South Korea as an adoptee as a baby. "So, the idea of having another family other than my birth family ties right into that as well. And then also, when it comes to my API (Asian Pacific Islander) identity, my lack of connection or non-connection to Asian culture really has isolated myself and many other adoptees from the API family. We're often outsiders looking in, even though it's our own racial and ethnic minority group. It really highlights the theme of family and what that means for me as I've navigated my own growth in my career and my interpersonal relationships. I feel very strongly about family, and at the same time, it can be a source of a lot of heartbreak for many."

Like Stephen, we all carry visible and invisible burdens shaped by our circumstances and experiences. However, only some of us have the inequities of our societal systems piled upon us in the workplace. That may look like the daily sting of microaggressions or the financial burden of being looked over for leadership positions layered on top of the things they may be facing in their personal lives. Yet, through it all, including the unspoken requirement for minority workers to work harder than their non-minority counterparts, Stephen says he still has grace for others. "When you lose sight of grace and empathy, you've lost touch with the humanity of it all. And what we are left with is a shell that is driven by one or two things, whether it's money or power."

The shared experience of hardship makes compassion more than just an act of kindness. It is our moral responsibility because when we offer grace to one another, we create space for our commonalities. Compassion calls us to see beyond ourselves, offer help, or stand in solidarity. Each of us can play a part in lightening the collective load by treating others with patience, empathy, and respect. When we acknowledge that life can be challenging for all of us, our interconnectedness can become a powerful antidote.

THE IMPACT OF HUMANITY

Truth DEI senior consultant David Dixon has one of the greatest stories of humanity I have ever heard where, through the power of compassion and forgiveness, someone else's trauma became his gift and his blessing. "I caused a fatal car accident when I was nineteen years old," David said. "I fell asleep behind the wheel on the night before Thanksgiving. The young lady in the other car was twenty-one years old. She was about to be the first in her family to graduate from college, but she never made it out of the car."

David's accident occurred during his sophomore year of college, and the psychological and emotional effects forced him to drop out of school. "The legal part took three years," said David, "So the same week that my friends were graduating from University of Miami, I was in court facing the victim's family. My worst-case scenario was fifteen years in prison, but before going into the courtroom, her family asked to meet with me. They hugged me and gave me their forgiveness for the accident. They said to me, 'Our daughter was such a beautiful spirit that if God put her in your path this way, it was for a reason.' They told me that I was supposed to do something great with my life because her spirit was too bright to be used for anything else."

The grace the family showed David taught him the power of forgiveness and the lesson that getting to a place of forgiveness is really for oneself. "They needed to forgive me in order to move forward, but I gained from it, too," David said. "They asked me to make them two promises. The first was to go back to school and finish my degree in her memory. The second was to make a difference with my life. I promised them that I would do as they asked, and when we walked back into the courtroom, they sat behind me. When the judge called my case, the mother stood up and made a statement asking the judge for leniency on my behalf."

David calls the family and their daughter angels in his life. The judge showed him leniency, and he could return to school, where he double-majored in psychology and business. "I earned two degrees, and I called the family to tell them that I got one for me and one for their daughter."

The truth about DEI is that it is both a human and business imperative and will remain so until systemic inequities are eliminated and the concept of equality has real meaning. As business leaders, we can all make the changes we need to see in our workplaces if we choose to. Do you really care about the people who work for you? If so, the choice should be an easy one. Let's do the work and move our society towards a future where fairness, equity, respect, and inclusion are ingrained in our workplaces and our communities.

As we end this book, I challenge you to do one thing to get started. Close the book, put it down, and talk with someone you don't know, whether it's your co-worker, your neighbor, or the person who delivers your packages. And it doesn't have to be a conversation about your differences. How about bridging the gap by focusing on your commonalities and taking the opportunity to learn from each other?

Endnotes

INTRODUCTION

1. "Equity, diversity, and inclusion." American Psychological Association website, accessed March 24, 2025, https://www.apa.org/topics/equity-diversity-inclusion.

CHAPTER 2

1. "The Transatlantic Slave Trade." Equal Justice Initiative website, accessed March 22, 2025, https://eji.org/reports/transatlantic-slave-trade-overview/.

2. "Fugitive Slave Acts." Britannica website, accessed March 22, 2025, https://www.britannica.com/event/Fugitive-Slave-Acts.

3. Harold Schindler. "The Bear River Massacre: New Historical Evidence." Brigham Young University website, accessed March 22, 2025, https://rsc.byu.edu/civil-war-saints/bear-river-massacre-new-historical-evidence.

4. "Indian Reservations." History.com website, accessed March 22, 2025, https://www.history.com/topics/native-american-history/indian-reservations.

5. Terry Anderson and Dominic Parker. "Un-American Reservations." Property and Environment Research Center website, accessed March 22, 2025, https://www.perc.org/2011/02/24/un-american-reservations/.

6. "Indian Adoption Project." The Adoption History Project website, accessed March 22, 2025, https://pages.uoregon.edu/adoption/topics/IAP.html.

7. "Indian Child Welfare Act." U.S. Department of the Interior Indian Affairs website, accessed March 22, 2025, https://www.bia.gov/bia/ois/dhs/icwa.

8. "Overview of the Holocaust: 1933–1945." Anti-Defamation League website, accessed March 22, 2025, https://www.adl.org/sites/default/files/overview-of-the-holocaust-nylm-guide.pdf.

9. Smith, David Livingstone, interview by Neal Conan, Talk of the Nation, NPR, March 29, 2011, https://www.npr.org/transcripts/134956180.

10. "Antisemitism Explained." United States Holocaust Memorial Museum website, accessed March 22, 2025, https://www.ushmm.org/antisemitism/what-is-antisemitism/explained.

11. U.S. Department of Justice. "Jury Recommends Sentence of Death for Pennsylvania Man Convicted for Tree of Life Synagogue Shooting." August 2, 2023, https://www.justice.gov/archives/opa/pr/jury-recommends-sentence-death-pennsylvania-man-convicted-tree-life-synagogue-shooting.

12. "Japanese Internment Camps." History.com website, accessed March 22, 2025, https://www.history.com/topics/world-war-ii/japanese-american-relocation.

13. "The Federal Constitutional Court Rules on the Constitutionality of Paragraph 175 (1957)." German History in Documents and Images website, accessed March 22, 2025, https://germanhistorydocs. org/en/occupation-and-the-emergence-of-two-states-1945-1961/ the-federal-constitutional-court-rules-on-the-constitutionality-of-paragraph-175-1957.

CHAPTER 3

1. "Dismantling DEI: A Coordinated Attack on American Values." Movement Advancement Project website, accessed March 22, 2025, https://www.mapresearch.org/file/2024-DEI-report-MAP.pdf.

2. Shirin Faqiri. "Alabama Gov. Kay Ivey signs sweeping law that prohibits diversity, equity, and inclusion at public schools and universities." CNN website, March 20, 2024, accessed March 22, 2025, https://www.cnn.com/2024/03/19/us/alabama-bill-bans-dei-public-universities-reaj/index.html.

3. Rebecca Griesbach. "Alabama Gov. Kay Ivey signs DEI bill into law: What the 'divisive concepts' ban will do." Advance Local website, March 20, 2024, accessed March 22, 2025, https://www.al.com/ news/2024/03/alabama-gov-kay-ivey-signs-dei-bill-into-law-what-the-divisive-concepts-ban-will-do.html.

4. "Ku Klux Klan." History.com website, accessed March 22, 2025, https://www.history.com/topics/19th-century/ku-klux-klan.

5. "Japanese Internment and Redress." United States House of Representatives History, Art & Archives website, accessed March 22, 2025, https://history.house.gov/Education/NHD/NHD-2025/ NHD-Internment/.

6. Michael Levin, Linda Gottfredson, and Roger Pearson. "White Nationalist." The Southern Poverty Law Center website, accessed March 22, 2025, https://www.splcenter.org/resources/extremist-files/white-nationalist/#:~:text=White%20nationalist%20groups%20espouse%20white%20supremacist%20or%20white,and%20even%20the%20victims%20of%20a%20racial%20genocide.

7. "Timeline of Legal History of Women in the United States." National Women's History Alliance website, accessed March 22, 2025, https://nationalwomenshistoryalliance.org/resources/womens-rights-movement/detailed-timeline/.

8. Heen, Mary L. "Agency: Married Women Traders of Nantucket: 1765–1865." *The Georgetown Journal of Gender and the Law* 21, no. 35 (2019): 35–93, https://www.law.georgetown.edu/gender-journal/wp-content/uploads/sites/20/2020/01/Article-3.pdf.

9. "Seneca Falls Convention." Britannica website, accessed March 22, 2025, https://www.britannica.com/event/Seneca-Falls-Convention.

10. "Equal Pay Act of 1963." U.S. Equal Employment Opportunity Commission website, accessed March 22, 2025, https://www.eeoc.gov/statutes/equal-pay-act-1963.

11. Cheyanne M. Daniels. "Multicultural Americans to become majority population by 2050: Report." *The Hill* website, January 17, 2024, accessed March 22, 2025, https://thehill.com/homenews/4412311-multicultural-americans-majority-population-2050/.

CHAPTER 5

1. Joe Hernandez. "White-sounding names get called back for jobs more than Black ones, a new study finds." NPR,

April 11, 2024, accessed March 22, 2025, https://www.npr.
org/2024/04/11/1243713272/resume-bias-study-white-names-
black-names.

CHAPTER 6

1. McIntosh, Peggy. "White Privilege: Unpacking the Invisible
   Knapsack." *Peace and Freedom* (July/August 1989), https://med.
   umn.edu/sites/med.umn.edu/files/2022-12/White-Privilege_
   McIntosh-1989.pdf.

CHAPTER 7

1. "Total population in the United States by gender from 2010 to
   2027." Statista website, accessed March 22, 2025, https://www.
   statista.com/statistics/737923/us-population-by-gender/.

2. Emma Hinchliffe. "The share of Fortune 500 companies run
   by women CEOs stays flat at 10.4% as pace of change stalls."
   Fortune, June 4, 2024, accessed March 22, 2025, https://fortune.
   com/2024/06/04/fortune-500-companies-women-ceos-2024/?utm_
   source=chatgpt.com.

3. Gracie Martinez and Jeffrey S. Passel. "Facts About the U.S. Black
   Population." Pew Research Center, January 23, 2025, accessed
   March 22, 2025, https://www.pewresearch.org/social-trends/
   fact-sheet/facts-about-the-us-black-population/.

4. Samantha Silberstein (reviewer). "Corporate Leadership by Race."
   Pro Invest News website, February 4, 2025, accessed March 22,
   2025, https://proinvestnews.com/2025/02/04/corporate-leadership-
   by-race/.

5. "New Estimates Highlight Differences in Growth Between the U.S. Hispanic and Non-Hispanic Population." United States Census Bureau, June 27, 2024, accessed March 22, 2025, https://www.census.gov/newsroom/press-releases/2024/population-estimates-characteristics.html.

6. Michael Volpe. "Meet the 16 Hispanic CEOs of the top S&P 500 Companies." Al Día website, February 3, 2021, accessed March 22, 2025, https://aldianews.com/en/leadership/advocacy/hispanics-sp-500.

7. Paige McGlauflin. "4 Fortune 500 companies are led by openly LGBTQ CEOs. Here's what they've said about their experience in corporate America." Yahoo! Finance website, June 6, 2023, accessed March 22, 2025, https://finance.yahoo.com/news/4-fortune-500-companies-led-100000173.html?guce_referrer=aHR0cHM6Ly93d3cuYmluZy5jb20v&guce_referrer_sig =AQAAAJ2nuMut82uMBNEPlsqyPfXJjLbm5 0dzLp6JHIQ-qaxO7Re3neTVYJf51LKzt WtypyI1Egvw5-KIc3djq7I6xKuXppy7LMLkXhf4_quBnXOGVNINyUbdxari-FXgcFGnhE-0nrH3yfBMuYir115uCeDkPP8q70wqobnCG6Pqao Vm&guccounter=2.

8. "2023 Annual Performance Report." U.S. Equal Employment Opportunity Commission website, February 23, 2024, accessed March 22, 2025, https://www.eeoc.gov/2023-annual-performance-report.

9. "Equal Pay Act of 1963." U. S. Equal Employment Opportunity Commission website, accessed March 22, 2025, https://www.eeoc.gov/statutes/equal-pay-act-1963.

10. Rakesh Kochhar. "The Enduring Grip of the Gender Pay Gap." Pew Research Center website, March 1, 2023, accessed March 22, 2025, https://www.pewresearch.org/social-trends/2023/03/01/the-enduring-grip-of-the-gender-pay-gap/.

11. Ibid.

12. Kerith J. Conron and Shoshana K. Goldberg. "LGBT People in the US Not Protected by State Non-Discrimination Statutes." UCLA School of Law Williams Institute website, April 2020, accessed March 24, 2025, https://williamsinstitute.law.ucla.edu/publications/lgbt-nondiscrimination-statutes/.

13. Brad Sears, Neko Michelle, Castleberry, Andy Lin, and Christy Mallory. "LGBTQ People's Experiences of Workplace Discrimination and Harassment." UCLA School of Law Williams Institute website, August 2024, accessed March 22, 2025, https://www.pewresearch.org/social-trends/2023/03/01/the-enduring-grip-of-the-gender-pay-gap/.

14. Trudy Ring. "82% of trans workers have suffered discrimination or harassment: report." Advocate website, November 21, 2024, accessed March 22, 2025, https://www.advocate.com/news/transgender-workplace-discrimination.

15. Trudy Ring. "Study Reveals 'Clear Bias' Against Nonbinary Job Applicants." Advocate website, February 8, 2023, accessed March 22, 2025, https://www.advocate.com/business/nonbinary-job-applicants.

16. "EEOC Sues Three Employers for Race Discrimination." U.S. Equal Employment Opportunity Commission website, October 1, 2024, accessed March 22, 2025, https://www.advocate.com/business/nonbinary-job-applicants.

17. "EEOC Increases Litigation Activity as Discrimination Statistics Rise." *Los Angeles Times* website, August 25, 2024, accessed March 22, 2025, https://www.latimes.com/b2b/consumer-attorneys-of-southern-california-2024/story/2024-08-25/eeoc-increases-litigation-activity-as-discrimination-statistics-rise.

CHAPTER 9

1. Conor Murray and Molly Bohannon. "MLB Removes References To Diversity From Careers Website: Here Are All The Companies Rolling Back DEI Programs." *Forbes*, March 22, 2025, access March 22, 2025, https://www.forbes.com/sites/conormurray/2025/03/22/mlb-removes-references-to-diversity-from-careers-website-here-are-all-the-companies-rolling-back-dei-programs/.

2. "U.S. Census Bureau Projections Show a Slower Growing, Older, More Diverse Nation a Half Century from Now." United States Census Bureau, December 12, 2012, accessed March 22, 2025, https://www.census.gov/newsroom/releases/archives/population/cb12-243.html.

3. Conor Murray and Molly Bohannon. "MLB Removes References To Diversity From Careers Website: Here Are All The Companies Rolling Back DEI Programs." *Forbes*, March 22, 2025, access March 22, 2025, https://www.forbes.com/sites/conormurray/2025/03/22/mlb-removes-references-to-diversity-from-careers-website-here-are-all-the-companies-rolling-back-dei-programs/.

4. Ibid.

5. Michaela Jeffery-Morrison. "Attracting And Retaining Gen-Z Through Diversity And Inclusion." *Forbes*, June 9, 2023, accessed March 22, 2025, https://www.forbes.com/councils/

forbesbusinesscouncil/2023/06/09/attracting-and-retaining-gen-z-through-diversity-and-inclusion/.

6. J. Merritt Melancon. "Consumer buying power is more diverse than ever." UGA Today, August 11, 2021, accessed March 22, 2025, https://news.uga.edu/selig-multicultural-economy-report-2021/#:~:text=The%20buying%20power%20of%20African%20Americans%20rose%20to,or%209%25%20of%20the%20nation's%20total%20buying%20power.

7. "US LGBTQ Spending Surpasses 1.4 Trillion Dollars in 2021 – According to the Pride Co-op." Yahoo! Finance, March 28, 2022, accessed March 22, 2025, https://finance.yahoo.com/news/us-lgbtq-spending-surpasses-1-205100102.html.

8. Sandy Carter. "Who Runs The World? Women Control 85% Of Purchases, 29% Of STEM Roles." *Forbes*, March 7, 2024, accessed March 22, 2025, https://finance.yahoo.com/news/us-lgbtq-spending-surpasses-1-205100102.html.

9. Ernesto Castañeda. "Proof that immigrants fuel the US economy is found in the billions they send back home." The Conversation website, October 24, 2024, accessed March 22, 2025, https://theconversation.com/proof-that-immigrants-fuel-the-us-economy-is-found-in-the-billions-they-send-back-home-227542.

10. Mike Schneider. "The US Census Bureau is adding refugees to its immigrant count." The Associated Press website, December 19, 2024, accessed March 22, 2025, https://apnews.com/article/immigrants-migration-census-bureau-cb4dddebad209cf14fac63e264825e0b.

About the Author

Nona Lee grew up loving sports. She medaled in the Junior Olympics for swimming and later played basketball at Pepperdine University, where she earned a bachelor's degree in broadcasting. Then, in law school, Lee obtained her juris doctor, graduated summa cum laude, and was awarded Graduate of the Year. Nona has also received certifications in Leadership for Corporate Counsel from Harvard University, as well as a Diversity, Equity, and Inclusion certification from Cornell University.

Lee dreamed of one day combining her practice as an attorney with her passion for sports, so she worked to become the first-ever associate general counsel for the Phoenix Suns professional basketball team. Lee later founded the Phoenix Women's Sports Association as a platform for helping girls and women find their power through sports. Later, Lee started the legal department for the Arizona Diamondbacks, where she became the team's first vice president and general counsel. At the time, she was only one of three women to hold this position with Major League Baseball

(MLB) clubs. At the time she left the D-backs in 2022, she was the only openly gay and only Black woman to hold an executive vice president position in all thirty of the MLB clubs.

Lee encountered countless acts of racism and discrimination while growing up in Los Angeles, during college, throughout law school, in her workplaces, and still today, being an openly gay, Black woman. Lee knew it was time to speak her truth and work to empower organizations and their leaders with diversity, equity, and inclusion knowledge and strategies to lead organizations through transformative change, so she founded Truth DEI Consulting, where she consults corporations around the country on diversity, equity, and inclusion for lasting change.

Lee is also the co-founder of Truth Retreats, a civil rights tour combined with diversity, equity, inclusion, and justice education, providing a transformative truth and reconciliation experience in Montgomery and Selma, Alabama. Truth Retreats is the only company that provides a civil rights trail tour along with the DEI tools needed to process your experience and develop a strategy for what you can do next in your community and workplace.

Lee has served on many boards, including the Board of Advisors for the National Sports Law Institute at Marquette University Law School, the Arizona State University Sports Law and Business Program advisory board, Trustee Emeritus for the Women's Sports Foundation; and past president and board member of the Sports Lawyers Association's Diversity, Equity, and Inclusion Committee, being the second woman president in its forty-plus-year history, the first woman of color, and first openly gay person to serve; board member and co-chair of the DEI Committee for the

National LGBTQ+ Bar Association; and a panelist on the NCAA's Independent Accountability Resolution Panel, hearing NCAA infractions cases.

Lee is a sought-after DEI consultant and keynote speaker, working with organizations such as Disney, Fresh Start, Alliance of Arizona Nonprofits, JAMS, Major Lindsey Africa, and more. Lee's mission is to create meaningful, lasting change in the world through diversity, equity, and inclusion education.